Algorithms

C

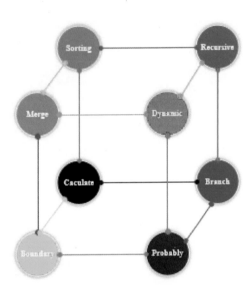

YANG HU

Simple is the beginning of wisdom. From the essence of practice, this book to briefly explain the concept and vividly cultivate programming interest, you will learn it easy and fast.

http://en.verejava.com

ISBN: 9798673993927

CONTENTS

Linear Table Definition

Linear Table:
Sequence of elements, is a one-dimensional array.

1. Define a one-dimensional array of student scores

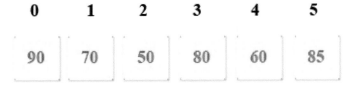

length = 6

TestOneArray.c

```c
#include <stdio.h>

int main()
{
    int scores[] = { 90, 70, 50, 80, 60, 85 };

    int length = sizeof(scores) / sizeof(scores[0]);
    int i;
    for (i = 0; i < length; i++)
    {
        printf("%d,", scores[i]);
    }

    return 0;
}
```

Result:

90,70,50,80,60,85,

Bubble Sorting Algorithm

Bubble Sorting Algorithm:
Compare arrays[j] with arrays[j + 1], if arrays[j] > arrays[j + 1] are exchanged. Remaining elements repeat this process, until sorting is completed.

Sort the following numbers from small to large

60   50   95   80   70

Explanation:

 No sorting,

 Comparing,

 Already sorted

1. First sorting:

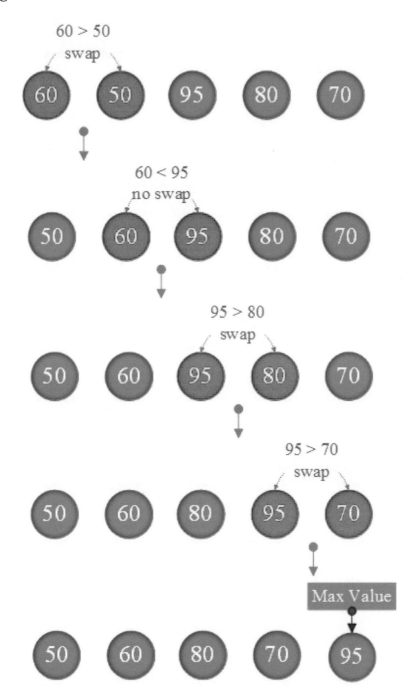

2. Second sorting:

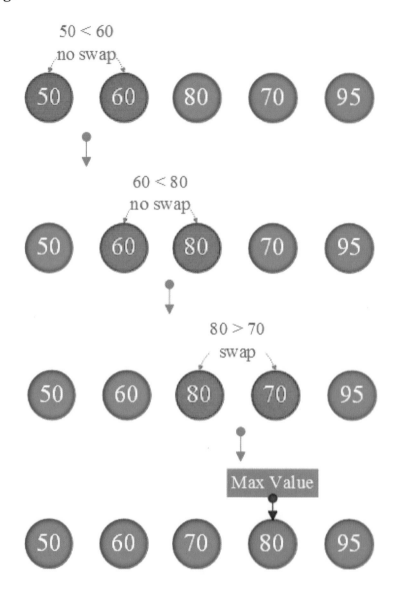

3. Third sorting:

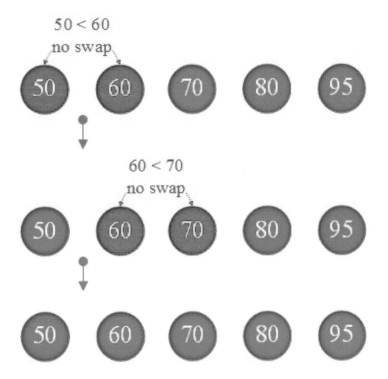

No swap so terminate sorting : **we can get the sorting numbers from small to large**

TestBubbleSort.c

```c
#include <stdio.h>
#define TRUE 1
#define FALSE 0
int main()
{
    int scores[] = { 90, 70, 50, 80, 60, 85 };
    int length = sizeof(scores) / sizeof(scores[0]);

    sort(scores, length);
    int i;
    for (i = 0; i < length; i++)
    {
        printf("%d,", scores[i]);
    }
    return 0;
}

void sort(int arrays[], int length)
{
    int i;
    int j;
    for (i = 0; i < length - 1; i++)
    {
        int isSwap = FALSE;
        for (j = 0; j < length - i - 1; j++)
        {
            if (arrays[j] > arrays[j + 1]) // exchange
            {
                int flag = arrays[j];
                arrays[j] = arrays[j + 1];
                arrays[j + 1] = flag;
                isSwap = TRUE;
            }
        }
        if(!isSwap) // No swap so stop sorting
        {
            break;
        }
    }
}
```

Result:
50,60,70,80,85,90,

Minimum Value

Search the Minimum of Integer Sequences:

1. Algorithmic ideas

Initial value minIndex=0, j=1 Compare arrays[minIndex] with arrays[j]
if arrays[minIndex] > arrays[j] then minIndex=j, j++ else j++. continue until the last number,
arrays[minIndex] is the Min Value.

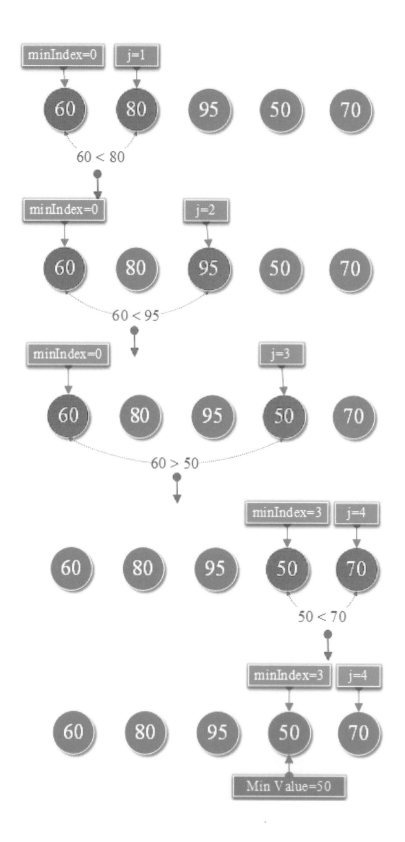

TestMinValue.c

```c
#include <stdio.h>

int min(int arrays[], int length)
{
    int minIndex = 0;// the index of the minimum
    int j;
    for (j = 1; j < length; j++)
    {
        if (arrays[minIndex] > arrays[j])
        {
            minIndex = j;
        }
    }
    return arrays[minIndex];
}

int main()
{
    int scores[] = { 60, 80, 95, 50, 70 };
    int length = sizeof(scores) / sizeof(scores[0]);
    int minValue = min(scores, length);
    printf("Min Value =   %d\n", minValue);
}
```

Result:

Min Value = 50

Select Sorting Algorithm

Select Sorting Algorithm:
Sorts an array by repeatedly finding the minimum element from unsorted part and putting it at the beginning.

Sort the following numbers from small to large

Explanation:

 No sorting,

 Comparing,

 Already sorted.

1. First sorting:

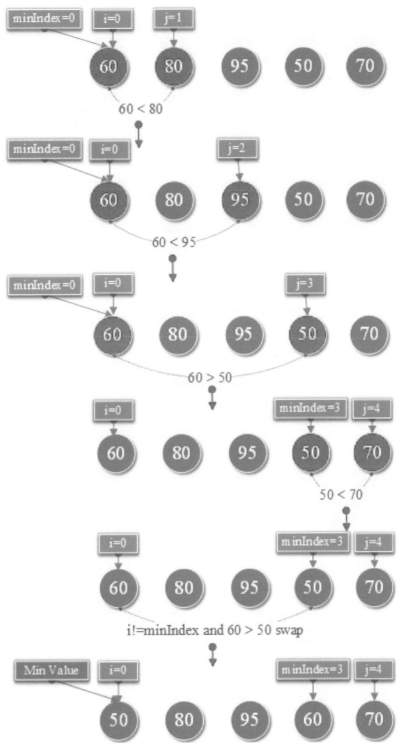

2. Second sorting:

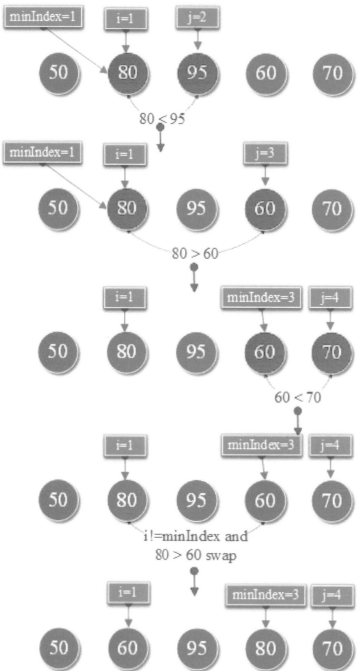

3. Third sorting:

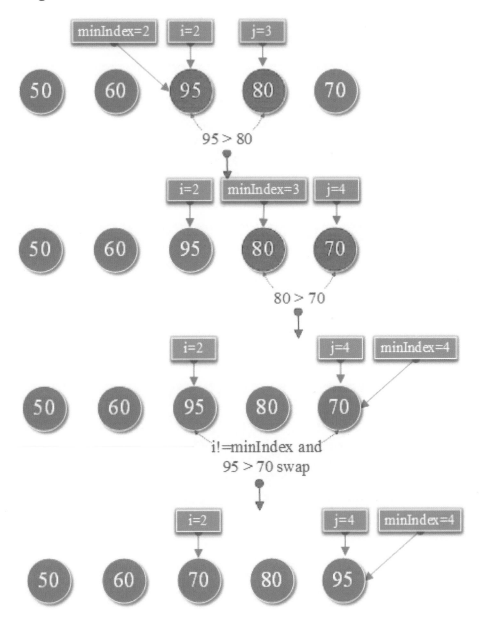

4. Forth sorting:

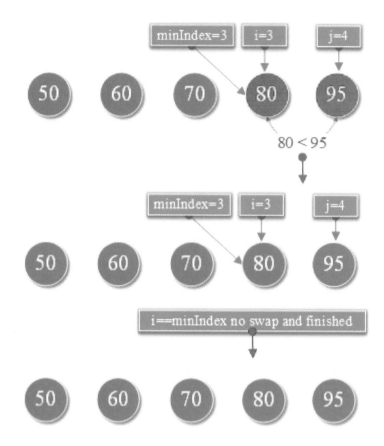

we can get the sorting numbers from small to large

TestSelectSort.c

```c
#include <stdio.h>
int main()
{
    int scores[] = { 90, 70, 50, 80, 60, 85 };
    int length = sizeof(scores) / sizeof(scores[0]);
    sort(scores, length);
    int i;
    for (i = 0; i < length; i++)
    {
        printf("%d,", scores[i]);
    }
    return 0;
}

void sort(int arrays[], int length)
{
    int minIndex;// Save the index of the selected minimum
    int i;
    int j;
    for (i = 0; i < length - 1; i++)
    {
        minIndex = i;
        int minValue = arrays[minIndex];
        for (j = i; j < length - 1; j++)
        {
            if (minValue > arrays[j + 1]) // minimum exchange with minIndex
            {
                minValue = arrays[j + 1];
                minIndex = j + 1;
            }
        }

        if (i != minIndex) // minimum is exchanged with the minIndex
        {
            int temp = arrays[i];
            arrays[i] = arrays[minIndex];
            arrays[minIndex] = temp;
        }
    }
}
```

Result:
50,60,70,80,85,90,

Linear Table Append

1. Add a score 75 to the end of the one-dimensional array scores.

Original Array Scores

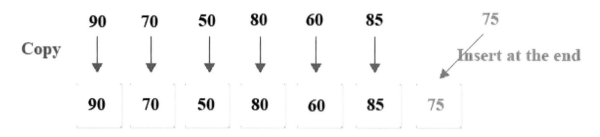

Analysis:
1. First create a temporary array(tempArray) larger than the original scores array length
2. Copy each value of the scores to tempArray
3. Assign 75 to the last index position of tempArray
4. Finally assign the tempArray pointer reference to the original scores;

TestOneArrayAppend.c

```c
#include <stdio.h>
#include <string.h>

int main()
{
    int scores[] = { 90, 70, 50, 80, 60, 85 };

    int length = sizeof(scores) / sizeof(scores[0]);
    int i;
    int tempArray[length + 1]; //create a new array

    for (i = 0; i < length; i++)
    {
        tempArray[i] = scores[i];
    }
    tempArray[length] = 75;

    memcpy(scores,tempArray,sizeof(tempArray));

    for (i = 0; i < length + 1; i++)
    {
        printf("%d,", scores[i]);
    }

    return 0;
}
```

Result:

90,70,50,80,60,85,75,

Linear Table Insert

1. Insert a student's score anywhere in the one-dimensional array scores.

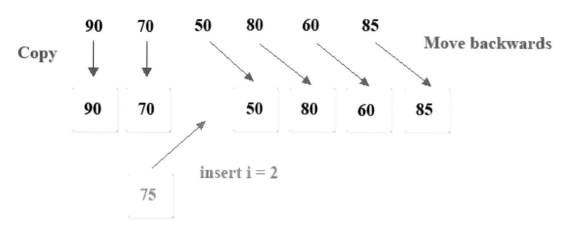

Analysis:
1. First create a temporary array tempArray larger than the original scores array length
2. Copy each value of the previous value of the scores array from the beginning to the insertion position to tempArray
3. Move the scores array from the insertion position to each value of the last element and move it back to tempArray
4. Then insert the score 75 to the index of the tempArray.
5. Finally assign the tempArray pointer reference to the scores;

TestOneArrayInsert.c

```c
#include <stdio.h>
#include <string.h>

int main()
{
    int scores[] = { 90, 70, 50, 80, 60, 85 };
    int length = sizeof(scores) / sizeof(scores[0]);
    int tempArray[length + 1];

    insert(scores, length, tempArray, 75, 2); //Insert 75 into the index = 2

    memcpy(scores,tempArray,sizeof(tempArray));

    int i;
    for (i = 0; i < length + 1; i++)
    {
        printf("%d,", scores[i]);
    }
    return 0;
}

void insert(int array[], int length, int tempArray[], int score, int insertIndex)
{
    int i;
    for (i = 0; i < length; i++)
    {
        if (i < insertIndex)
        {
            tempArray[i] = array[i];
        }
        else
        {
            tempArray[i + 1] = array[i];
        }
    }
    tempArray[insertIndex] = score;
}
```

Result:
90,70,75,50,80,60,85,

Linear Table Delete

1. Delete the value of the index=2 from scores array

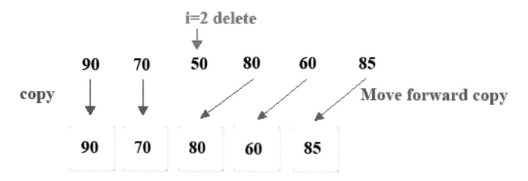

Analysis:

1. Create a temporary array tempArray that length smaller than scores by 1.
2. Copy the data in front of i=2 to the front of tempArray
3. Copy the array after i=2 to the end of tempArray
4. Assign the tempArray pointer reference to the scores
5. Printout scores

TestOneArrayDelete.c

```c
#include <stdio.h>
#include <string.h>

int main()
{
    int scores[] = { 90, 70, 50, 80, 60, 85 };
    printf("Please enter the index to be deleted: \n");
    int index;
    scanf("%d", &index);

    int length = sizeof(scores) / sizeof(scores[0]);
    int tempArray[length - 1]; // create a new array
    int i;
    for (i = 0; i < length; i++)
    {
        if (i < index) // Copy data in front of index to the front of tempArray
            tempArray[i] = scores[i];
        if (i > index)  // Copy the array after index to the end of tempArray
            tempArray[i - 1] = scores[i];
    }

    memcpy(scores,tempArray,sizeof(tempArray));

    for (i = 0; i < length - 1; i++)
    {
        printf("%d,", scores[i]);
    }

    return 0;
}
```

Result:

Please enter the index to be deleted:
2
90,70,80,60,85,

Insert Sorting Algorithm

Insert Sorting Algorithm:
Take an unsorted new element in the array, compare it with the already sorted element before, if the element is smaller than the sorted element, insert new element to the right position.

Sort the following numbers from small to large

Explanation:

 No sorting,

 Inserting,

 Already sorted

1. First sorting:

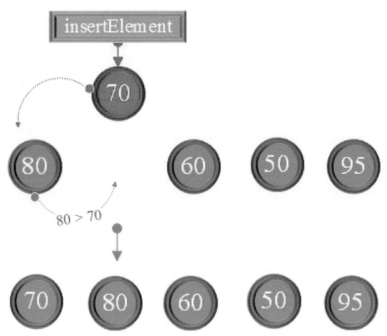

2. Second sorting:

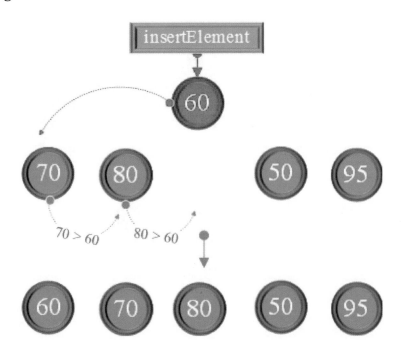

3. Third sorting:

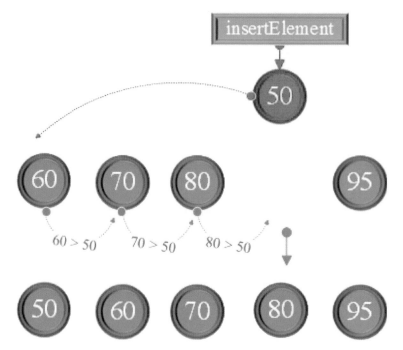

4 Third sorting:

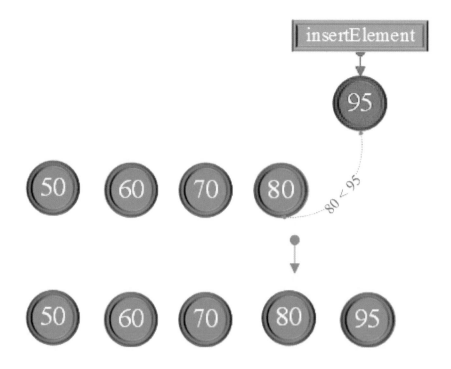

TestInsertSort.c

```c
#include <stdio.h>

int main()
{
    int scores[] = { 90, 70, 50, 80, 60, 85 };
    int length = sizeof(scores) / sizeof(scores[0]);

    sort(scores, length);

    int i;
    for (i = 0; i < length; i++)
    {
        printf("%d,", scores[i]);
    }
    return 0;
}

void sort(int arrays[], int length)
{
    int i;
    int j;
    for (i = 0; i < length; i++) {
        int insertElement = arrays[i];//Take unsorted new elements
        int insertPosition = i;
        for (j = insertPosition - 1; j >= 0; j--) {
            //If insertElement is smaller than the sorted element, shift to the right
            if (insertElement < arrays[j]) {
                arrays[j + 1] = arrays[j];
                insertPosition--;
            }
        }
        arrays[insertPosition] = insertElement;//Insert the new element
    }
}
```

Result:

50,60,70,80,85,90,

Reverse Array

Inversion of ordered sequences:

1. Algorithmic ideas

Initial $i = 0$ and then swap the first element arrays[i] with last element arrays[length - i - 1]
Repeat until index of middle $i == $ length / 2.

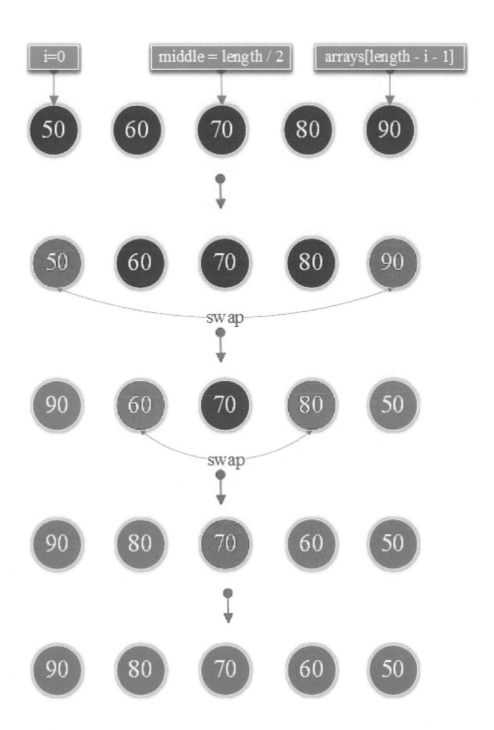

TestReverse.c

```c
#include <stdio.h>

void reverse(int arrays[], int length)
{
    int middle = length / 2;
    int i;
    for (i = 0; i <= middle; i++) {
        int temp = arrays[i];
        arrays[i] = arrays[length - i - 1];
        arrays[length - i - 1] = temp;
    }
}

int main()
{
    int scores[] = { 50, 60, 70, 80, 90 };
    int length = sizeof(scores) / sizeof(scores[0]);
    reverse(scores, length);
    int i;
    for (i = 0; i < length; i++)
    {
        printf("%d,", scores[i]);
    }
}
```

Result:

```
90,80,70,60,50,
```

Linear Table Search

1. Please enter the value you want to search like : 70 return index.

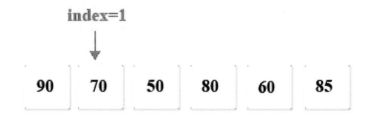

Analysis:

Traverse the value in the array scores, if there is a value equal to the given value like 70, print out the current index

TestOneArraySearch.c

```c
#include <stdio.h>
#include <string.h>

#define TRUE  1
#define FALSE 0

int main()
{
    int scores[] = { 90, 70, 50, 80, 60, 85 };
    printf("Please enter the value you want to search : \n");
    int value;
    scanf("%d", &value);

    int isSearch = FALSE;
    int length = sizeof(scores) / sizeof(scores[0]);
    int i;
    for (i = 0; i < length; i++)
    {
        if (scores[i] == value)
        {
            isSearch = TRUE;
            printf("Found value: %d the index is: %d", value, i);
            break;
        }
    }

    if (!isSearch)
    {
        printf("The value was not found : %d", value);
    }
    return 0;
}
```

Result:

Please enter the value you want to search :
70
Found value: 70 the index is: 1

Dichotomy Binary Search

Dichotomy Binary Search:
Find the index position of a given value from an already ordered array.

1. Initialize the lowest index low=0, the highest index high=scores.length-1
2. Find the searchValue of the middle index mid=(low+high)/2 scores[mid]
3. Compare the scores[mid] with searchValue
   If the scores[mid]==searchValue print current mid index,
   If scores[mid]>searchValue that the searchValue will be found between low and mid-1
4. And so on. Repeat step 3 until you find searchValue or low>=high to terminate the loop.

Example 1 : Find the index of searchValue=40 in the array that has been sorted below.

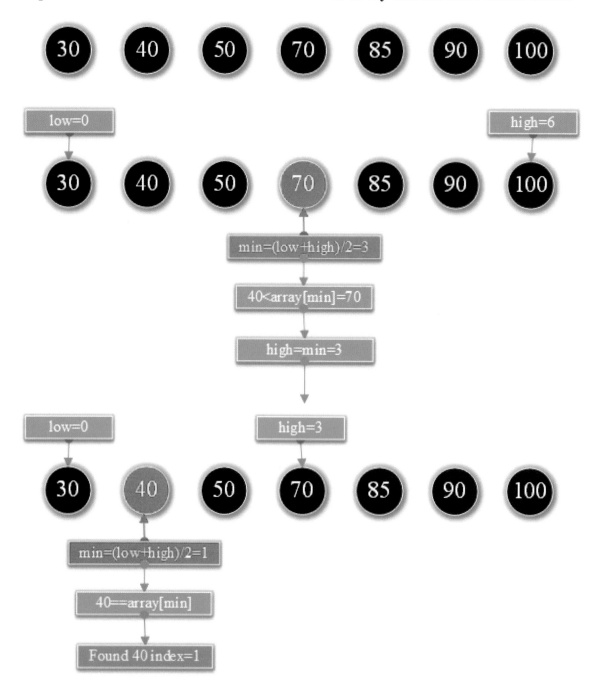

Example 2 : Find the index of searchValue=90 in the array that has been sorted below.

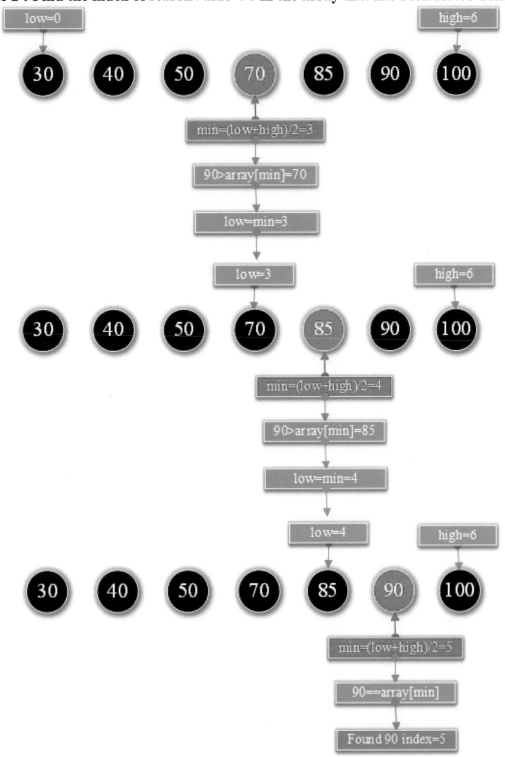

TestBinarySearch.c

```c
#include <stdio.h>
int main()
{
    int scores[] = { 30, 40, 50, 70, 85, 90, 100 };
    int length = sizeof(scores) / sizeof(scores[0]);

    int searchValue = 40;
    int position = binarySearch(scores, length, searchValue);
    printf("%d position : %d",searchValue, position);

    printf("\n--------------------------\n");

    searchValue = 90;
    position = binarySearch(scores, length, searchValue);
    printf("%d position : %d",searchValue, position);
    return 0;
}

int binarySearch(int arrays[], int length, int searchValue)
{
    int low = 0;
    int high = length;
    int mid = 0;
    while (low <= high)
    {
        mid = (low + high) / 2;
        if (arrays[mid] == searchValue)
        {
            return mid;
        }
        else if (arrays[mid] < searchValue)
        {
            low = mid + 1;
        }
        else if (arrays[mid] > searchValue)
        {
            high = mid - 1;
        }
    }
    return -1;
}
```

Result:

40 position:1

----

90 position:5

Shell Sorting

Shell Sorting:
Shell sort is a highly efficient sorting algorithm and is based on insertion sort algorithm. This algorithm avoids large shifts as in case of insertion sort, if the smaller value is to the far right and has to be moved to the far left.

Sort the following numbers from small to large by Shell Sorting

Algorithmic result:
The array is grouped according to a certain increment of subscripts, and the insertion of each group is sorted. As the increment decreases gradually until the increment is 1, the whole data is grouped and sorted.

# 1. The first sorting :
gap = array.length / 2 = 5

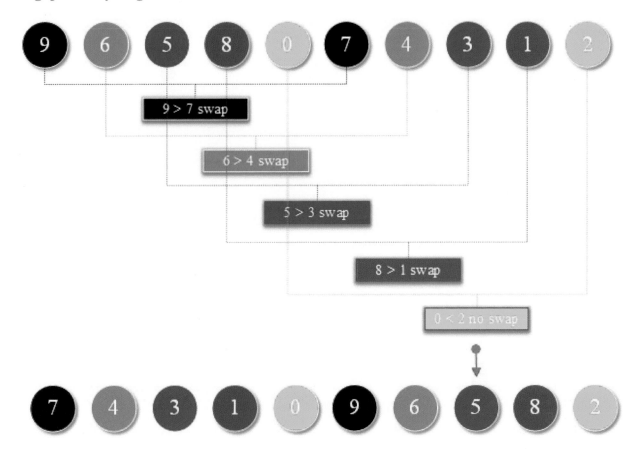

2. The second sorting :
gap = 5 / 2 = 2

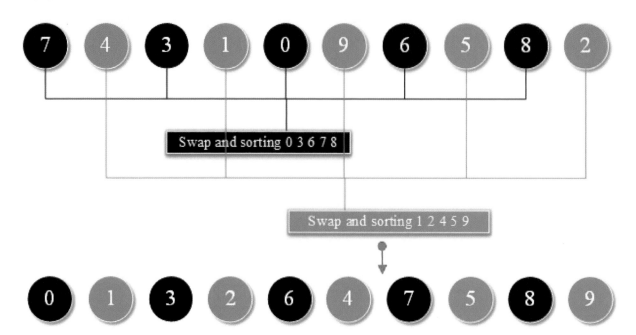

3. The third sorting :

gap = 2 / 2 = 1

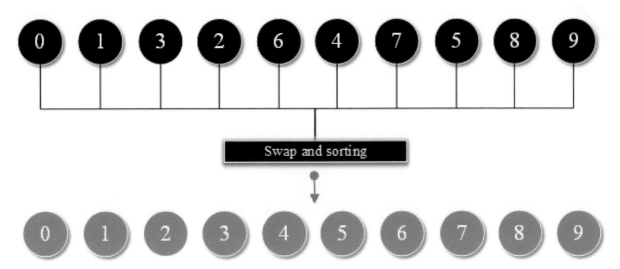

TestShellSort.c

```c
#include <stdio.h>

void swap(int array[], int a, int b)
{
    array[a] = array[a] + array[b];
    array[b] = array[a] - array[b];
    array[a] = array[a] - array[b];
}

void shellSort(int array[], int length)
{
    int gap;
    for (gap = length / 2; gap > 0; gap = gap / 2)
    {
        int i;
        for (i = gap; i < length; i++)
        {
            int j = i;
            while (j - gap >= 0 && array[j] < array[j - gap])
            {
                swap(array, j, j - gap);
                j = j - gap;
            }
        }
    }
}

int main()
{
    int scores[] = { 9, 6, 5, 8, 0, 7, 4, 3, 1, 2 };
    int length = sizeof(scores) / sizeof(scores[0]);
    shellSort(scores, length);
    int i;
    for (i = 0; i < length; i++)
    {
        printf("%d,", scores[i]);
    }
    return 0;
}
```

Result:
0,1,2,3,4,5,6,7,8,9,

Unidirectional Linked List

Unidirectional Linked List Single Link:
Is a chained storage structure of a linear table, which is connected by a node. Each node consists of data and next pointer to the next node.

UML Diagram

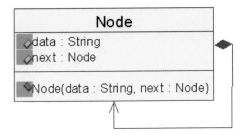

```
struct Node
{
   char data[50];
   struct Node *next;
}
```

1. Unidirectional Linked List initialization.

Example : Construct a San Francisco subway Unidirectional linked list

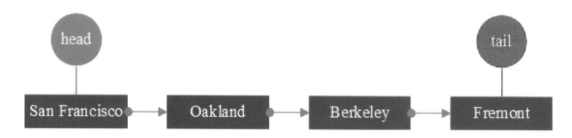

2. traversal output.

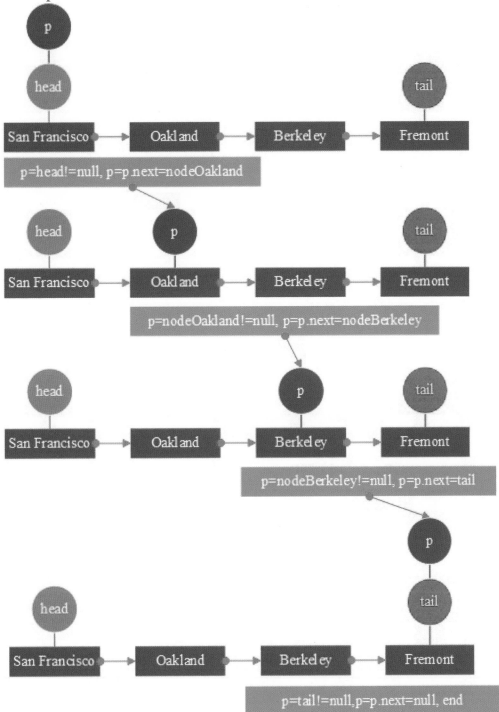

TestUnidirectionalLinkedList.c

```c
#include <stdio.h>
#include<stdlib.h>
#include <string.h>

typedef struct Node
{
    char data[50];
    struct Node *next;
} Node;

Node *head = NULL;

void init()
{
    // the first node called head node
    head = (Node*)malloc(sizeof(Node));
    strcpy(head->data, "San Francisco");
    head->next = NULL;

    Node *nodeOakland = NULL;
    nodeOakland = (Node*)malloc(sizeof(Node));
    strcpy(nodeOakland->data, "Oakland");
    nodeOakland->next = NULL;
    head->next = nodeOakland;

    Node *nodeBerkeley = NULL;
    nodeBerkeley = (Node*)malloc(sizeof(Node));
    strcpy(nodeBerkeley->data, "Berkeley");
    nodeBerkeley->next = NULL;
    nodeOakland->next = nodeBerkeley;

    // the last node called tail node
    Node *tail = NULL;
    tail = (Node*)malloc(sizeof(Node));
    strcpy(tail->data, "Fremont");
    tail->next = NULL;
    nodeBerkeley->next = tail;
}
```

```c
void output(Node *node)
{
    Node *p = node;

    while (p != NULL) // From the beginning to the end
    {
        printf("%s -> ", p->data);
        p = p->next;
    }
    printf("End\n\n");
}

void freeMemery()
{
    Node *p = head;
    Node *temp = p;

    while (p != NULL)
    {
        temp = p;
        p = p->next;
        free(temp);
    }
}

int main()
{
    init();
    output(head);
    freeMemery();

    return 0;
}
```

Result:

San Francisco -> Oakland -> Berkeley -> Fremont -> End

3. Append a new node name: Walnut to the end.

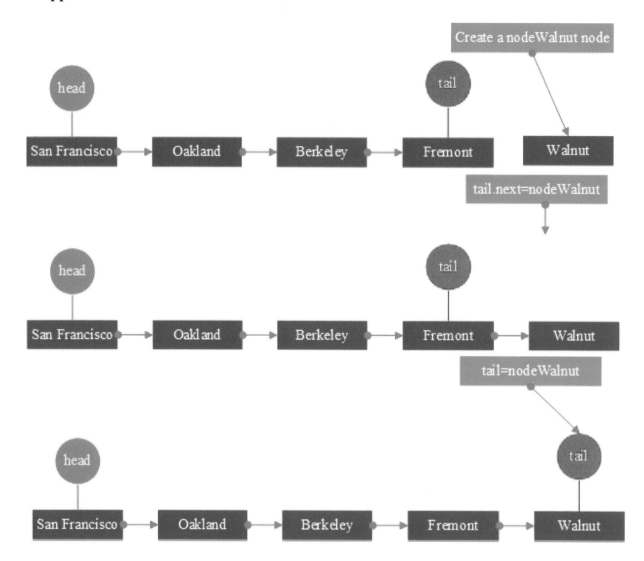

TestUnidirectionalLinkedList.c

```c
#include <stdio.h>
#include<stdlib.h>
#include <string.h>

typedef struct Node
{
   char data[50];
   struct Node *next;
} Node;

Node *head  = NULL;
Node *tail = NULL;

void init()
{
   // the first node called head node
   head = (Node*)malloc(sizeof(Node));
   strcpy(head->data, "San Francisco");
   head->next = NULL;

   Node *nodeOakland = NULL;
   nodeOakland = (Node*)malloc(sizeof(Node));
   strcpy(nodeOakland->data, "Oakland");
   nodeOakland->next = NULL;
   head->next = nodeOakland;

   Node *nodeBerkeley = NULL;
   nodeBerkeley = (Node*)malloc(sizeof(Node));
   strcpy(nodeBerkeley->data, "Berkeley");
   nodeBerkeley->next = NULL;
   nodeOakland->next = nodeBerkeley;

   // the last node called tail node
   tail = (Node*)malloc(sizeof(Node));
   strcpy(tail->data, "Fremont");
   tail->next = NULL;
   nodeBerkeley->next = tail;
}
```

```c
void add(char data[])
{
    Node *newNode = NULL;
    newNode = (Node*)malloc(sizeof(Node));
    strcpy(newNode->data, data);
    newNode->next = NULL;
    tail->next = newNode;
    tail = newNode;
}

void output(Node *node)
{
    Node *p = node;

    while (p != NULL) // From the beginning to the end
    {
        printf("%s -> ", p->data);
        p = p->next;
    }
    printf("End\n\n");
}

void freeMemery()
{
    Node *p = head;
    Node *temp = p;

    while (p != NULL)
    {
        temp = p;
        p = p->next;
        free(temp);
    }
}
```

```
int main()
{
    init();

    printf("Append a new node name: Walnut  to the end: \n");
    add("Walnut");

    output(head);
    freeMemery();

    return 0;
}
```

Result:

Append a new node name: Walnut to the end:
San Francisco -> Oakland -> Berkeley -> Fremont -> Walnut -> End

3. Insert a node Walnut in position 2.

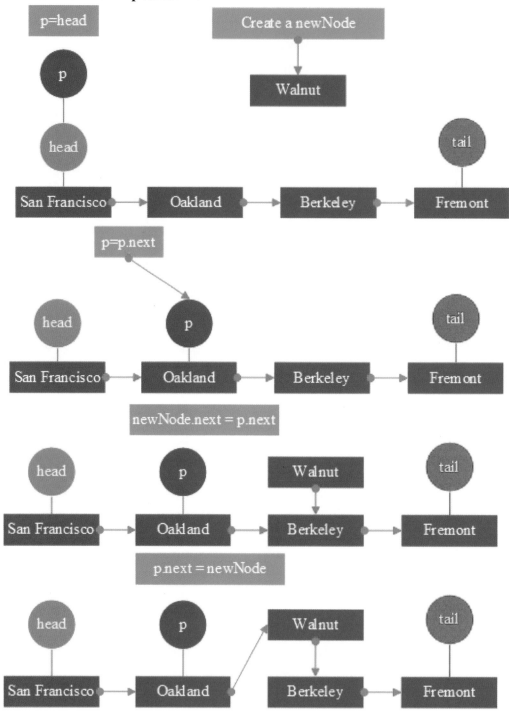

TestUnidirectionalLinkedList.c

```c
#include <stdio.h>
#include<stdlib.h>
#include <string.h>

typedef struct Node
{
   char data[50];
   struct Node *next;
} Node;

Node *head  = NULL;
Node *tail = NULL;

void init()
{
   head = (Node*)malloc(sizeof(Node));
   strcpy(head->data, "San Francisco");
   head->next = NULL;

   Node *nodeOakland = NULL;
   nodeOakland = (Node*)malloc(sizeof(Node));
   strcpy(nodeOakland->data, "Oakland");
   nodeOakland->next = NULL;
   head->next = nodeOakland;

   Node *nodeBerkeley = NULL;
   nodeBerkeley = (Node*)malloc(sizeof(Node));
   strcpy(nodeBerkeley->data, "Berkeley");
   nodeBerkeley->next = NULL;
   nodeOakland->next = nodeBerkeley;

   // the last node called tail node
   tail = (Node*)malloc(sizeof(Node));
   strcpy(tail->data, "Fremont");
   tail->next = NULL;
   nodeBerkeley->next = tail;
}
```

```c
void insert(int insertPosition, char data[])
{
    Node *p = head;
    int i = 0;
    // Move the node to the insertion position
    while (p->next != NULL && i < insertPosition - 1)
    {
        p = p->next;
        i++;
    }

    Node *newNode = NULL;
    newNode = (Node*)malloc(sizeof(Node));
    strcpy(newNode->data, data);
    newNode->next = p->next; // newNode next point to next node
    p->next = newNode; // current next point to newNode
}

void output(Node *node)
{
    Node *p = node;

    while (p != NULL) // From the beginning to the end
    {
        printf("%s -> ", p->data);
        p = p->next;
    }
    printf("End\n\n");
}

void freeMemery()
{
    Node *p = head;
    Node *temp = p;

    while (p != NULL)
    {
        temp = p;
        p = p->next;
        free(temp);
    }
}
```

```
int main()
{
    init();

    printf("Insert a new node Walnut at index = 2 : \n");
    insert(2, "Walnut");

    output(head);
    freeMemery();

    return 0;
}
```

Result:

Insert a new node Walnut at index = 2 :
San Francisco -> Oakland -> Walnut -> Berkeley -> Fremont -> End

4. Delete the index=2 node.

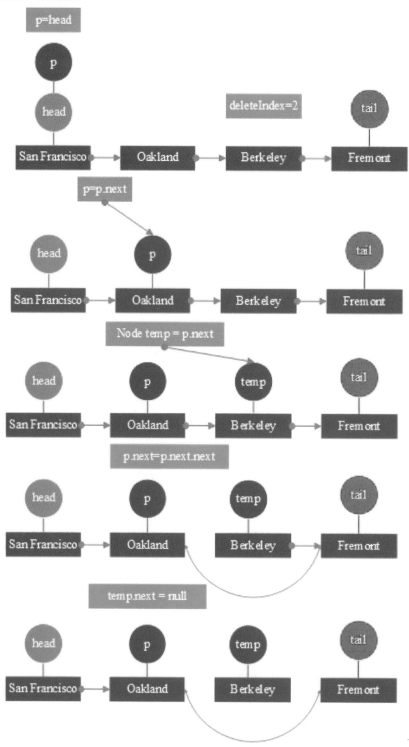

TestUnidirectionalLinkedList.c

```c
#include <stdio.h>
#include<stdlib.h>
#include <string.h>

typedef struct Node
{
   char data[50];
   struct Node *next;
} Node;

Node *head  = NULL;
Node *tail = NULL;

void init()
{
   head = (Node*)malloc(sizeof(Node));
   strcpy(head->data, "San Francisco");
   head->next = NULL;

   Node *nodeOakland = NULL;
   nodeOakland = (Node*)malloc(sizeof(Node));
   strcpy(nodeOakland->data, "Oakland");
   nodeOakland->next = NULL;
   head->next = nodeOakland;

   Node *nodeBerkeley = NULL;
   nodeBerkeley = (Node*)malloc(sizeof(Node));
   strcpy(nodeBerkeley->data, "Berkeley");
   nodeBerkeley->next = NULL;
   nodeOakland->next = nodeBerkeley;

   // the last node called tail node
   tail = (Node*)malloc(sizeof(Node));
   strcpy(tail->data, "Fremont");
   tail->next = NULL;
   nodeBerkeley->next = tail;
}
```

```c
void removeNode(int removePosition)
{
    Node *p = head;
    int i = 0;
    // Move the node to the previous node position that was deleted
    while (p->next != NULL && i < removePosition - 1)
    {
        p = p->next;
        i++;
    }

    Node *temp = p->next;// Save the node you want to delete
    p->next = p->next->next;// Previous node next points to next of delete the node
    temp->next = NULL;
    free(temp);
}

void output(Node *node)
{
    Node *p = node;

    while (p != NULL) // From the beginning to the end
    {
        printf("%s -> ", p->data);
        p = p->next;
    }
    printf("End\n\n");
}

void freeMemery()
{
    Node *p = head;
    Node *temp = p;

    while (p != NULL)
    {
        temp = p;
        p = p->next;
        free(temp);
    }
}
```

```c
int main()
{
    init();

    printf("Delete a new node Berkeley at index = 2 : \n");
    removeNode(2);

    output(head);
    freeMemery();

    return 0;
}
```

Result:

Delete a new node Berkeley at index = 2 :
San Francisco -> Oakland -> Fremont -> End

Doubly Linked List

Doubly Linked List:
It is a chained storage structure of a linear table. It is connected by nodes in two directions. Each node consists of data, pointing to the previous node and pointing to the next node.

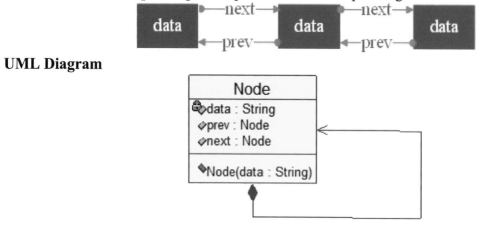

UML Diagram

```
typedef struct Node
{
    char data[50];
    struct Node *prev;
    struct Node *next;
} Node;
```

1. Doubly Linked List initialization.
Example : Construct a San Francisco subway Doubly linked list

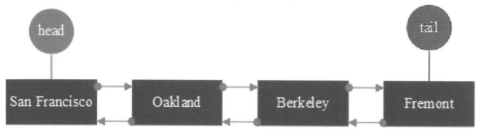

2. traversal output. TestDoubleLink.c

```c
#include <stdio.h>
#include<stdlib.h>
#include <string.h>

typedef struct Node
{
    char data[50];
    struct Node *prev;
    struct Node *next;
} Node;

Node *head  = NULL;
Node *tail = NULL;

void init()
{
    head = (Node*)malloc(sizeof(Node));
    strcpy(head->data, "San Francisco");
    head->prev = NULL;
    head->next = NULL;

    Node *nodeOakland = NULL;
    nodeOakland = (Node*)malloc(sizeof(Node));
    strcpy(nodeOakland->data, "Oakland");
    nodeOakland->prev = head;
    nodeOakland->next = NULL;
    head->next = nodeOakland;

    Node *nodeBerkeley = NULL;
    nodeBerkeley = (Node*)malloc(sizeof(Node));
    strcpy(nodeBerkeley->data, "Berkeley");
    nodeBerkeley->prev = nodeOakland;
    nodeBerkeley->next = NULL;
    nodeOakland->next = nodeBerkeley;

    tail = (Node*)malloc(sizeof(Node));
    strcpy(tail->data, "Fremont");
    tail->prev = nodeBerkeley;
    tail->next = NULL;
    nodeBerkeley->next = tail;
}
```

```c
void output(Node *node)
{
    Node *p = node;
    Node *end = NULL;
    while (p != NULL)
    {
        printf("%s -> ", p->data);
        end = p;
        p = p->next;
    }
    printf("End\n");

    p = end;
    while (p != NULL)
    {
        printf("%s -> ", p->data);
        p = p->prev;
    }
    printf("Start\n\n");
}

void freeMemery()
{
    Node *p = head;
    Node *temp = p;
    while (p != NULL)
    {
        temp = p;
        p = p->next;
        free(temp);
    }
}

int main()
{
    init();
    output(head);
    freeMemery();
    return 0;
}
```

Result:
San Francisco -> Oakland -> Berkeley -> Fremont -> End
Fremont -> Berkeley -> Oakland -> San Francisco -> Start

3. add a node Walnut at the end of Fremont.

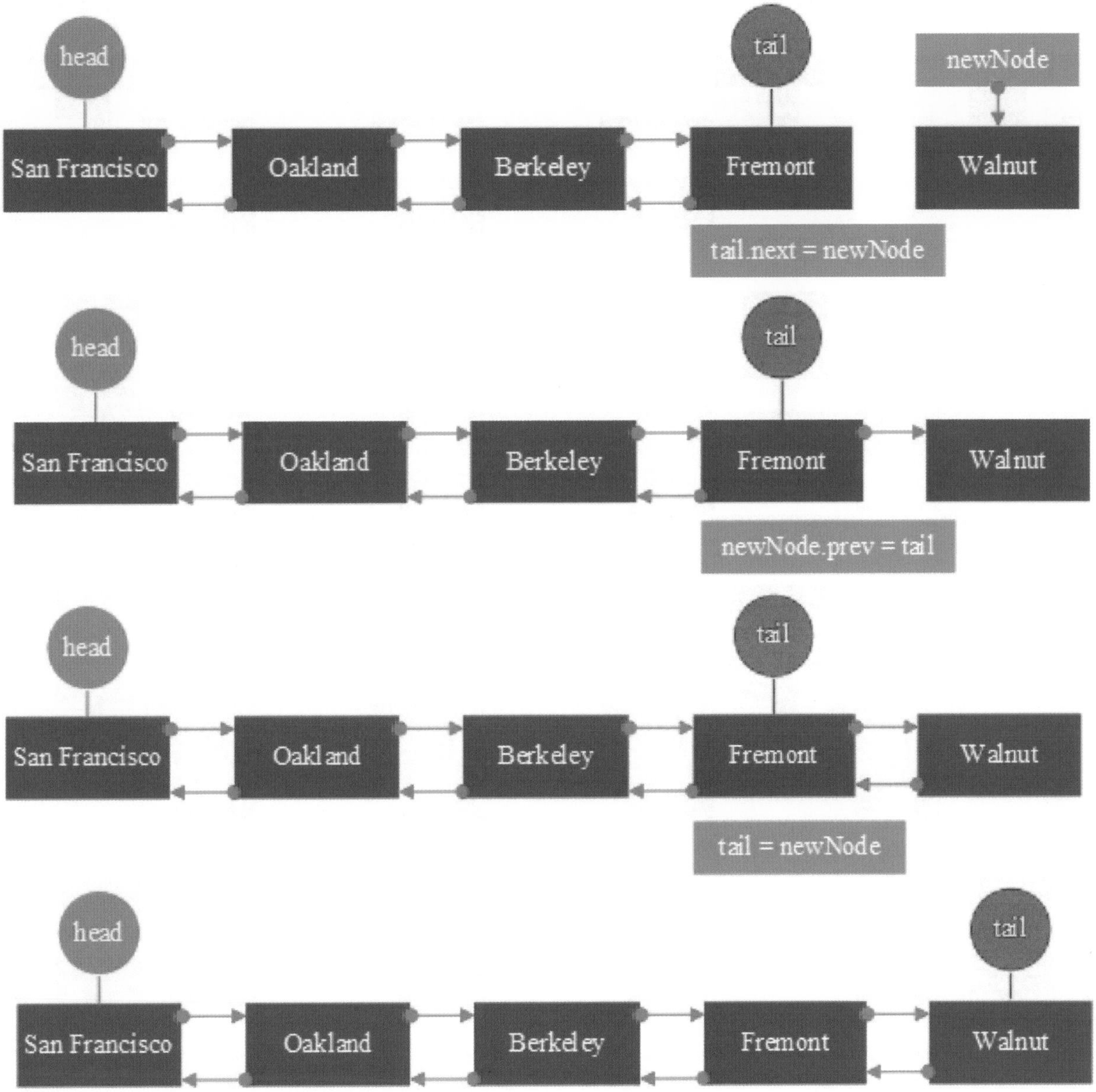

head → San Francisco ↔ Oakland ↔ Berkeley ↔ Fremont (tail)   newNode → Walnut

tail.next = newNode

head → San Francisco ↔ Oakland ↔ Berkeley ↔ Fremont (tail) → Walnut

newNode.prev = tail

head → San Francisco ↔ Oakland ↔ Berkeley ↔ Fremont (tail) ↔ Walnut

tail = newNode

head → San Francisco ↔ Oakland ↔ Berkeley ↔ Fremont ↔ Walnut (tail)

TestDoubleLink.c

```c
#include <stdio.h>
#include<stdlib.h>
#include <string.h>
typedef struct Node
{
    char data[50];
    struct Node *prev;
    struct Node *next;
} Node;

Node *head = NULL;
Node *tail = NULL;

void init()
{
    head = (Node*)malloc(sizeof(Node));
    strcpy(head->data, "San Francisco");
    head->prev = NULL;
    head->next = NULL;

    Node *nodeOakland = NULL;
    nodeOakland = (Node*)malloc(sizeof(Node));
    strcpy(nodeOakland->data, "Oakland");
    nodeOakland->prev = head;
    nodeOakland->next = NULL;
    head->next = nodeOakland;

    Node *nodeBerkeley = NULL;
    nodeBerkeley = (Node*)malloc(sizeof(Node));
    strcpy(nodeBerkeley->data, "Berkeley");
    nodeBerkeley->prev = nodeOakland;
    nodeBerkeley->next = NULL;
    nodeOakland->next = nodeBerkeley;

    tail = (Node*)malloc(sizeof(Node));
    strcpy(tail->data, "Fremont");
    tail->prev = nodeBerkeley;
    tail->next = NULL;
    nodeBerkeley->next = tail;
}
```

```c
void add(char data[])
{
    Node *newNode = NULL;
    newNode = (Node*)malloc(sizeof(Node));
    strcpy(newNode->data, data);
    newNode->next = NULL;
    tail->next = newNode;
    newNode->prev = tail;
    tail = newNode;
}

void output(Node *node)
{
    Node *p = node;
    Node *end = NULL;
    while (p != NULL)
    {
        printf("%s -> ", p->data);
        end = p;
        p = p->next;
    }
    printf("End\n");

    p = end;
    while (p != NULL)
    {
        printf("%s -> ", p->data);
        p = p->prev;
    }
    printf("Start\n\n");
}

void freeMemery()
{
    Node *p = head;
    Node *temp = p;
    while (p != NULL)
    {
        temp = p;
        p = p->next;
        free(temp);
    }
}
```

```
int main()
{
    init();

    printf("Add a new node Walnut : \n");
    add("Walnut");

    output(head);
    freeMemery();

    return 0;
}
```

Result:

San Francisco -> Oakland -> Berkeley -> Fremont -> Walnut -> End
Walnut -> Fremont -> Berkeley -> Oakland -> San Francisco -> Start

3. Insert a node Walnut in position 2.

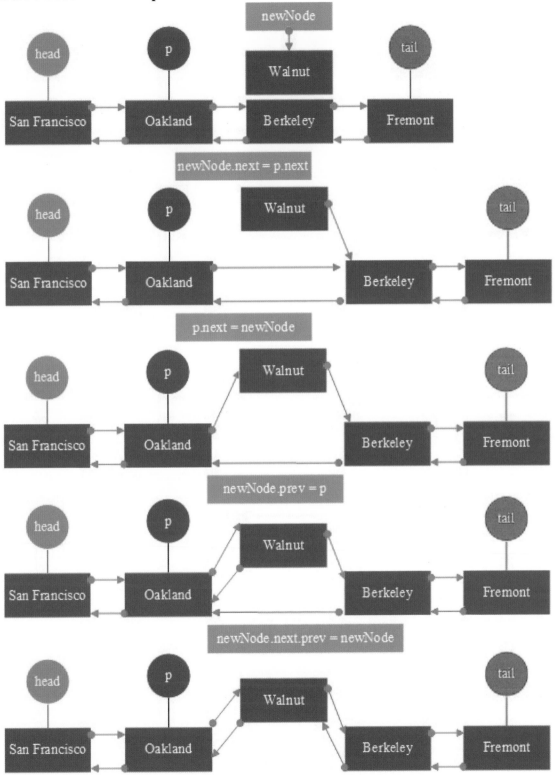

TestDoubleLink.c

```c
#include <stdio.h>
#include<stdlib.h>
#include <string.h>
typedef struct Node
{
    char data[50];
    struct Node *prev;
    struct Node *next;
} Node;

Node *head  = NULL;
Node *tail = NULL;

void init()
{
    head = (Node*)malloc(sizeof(Node));
    strcpy(head->data, "San Francisco");
    head->prev = NULL;
    head->next = NULL;

    Node *nodeOakland = NULL;
    nodeOakland = (Node*)malloc(sizeof(Node));
    strcpy(nodeOakland->data, "Oakland");
    nodeOakland->prev = head;
    nodeOakland->next = NULL;
    head->next = nodeOakland;

    Node *nodeBerkeley = NULL;
    nodeBerkeley = (Node*)malloc(sizeof(Node));
    strcpy(nodeBerkeley->data, "Berkeley");
    nodeBerkeley->prev = nodeOakland;
    nodeBerkeley->next = NULL;
    nodeOakland->next = nodeBerkeley;

    tail = (Node*)malloc(sizeof(Node));
    strcpy(tail->data, "Fremont");
    tail->prev = nodeBerkeley;
    tail->next = NULL;
    nodeBerkeley->next = tail;
}
```

```c
void insert(int insertPosition, char data[])
{
    Node *p = head;
    int i = 0;
    // Move the node to the insertion position
    while (p->next != NULL && i < insertPosition - 1)
    {
        p = p->next;
        i++;
    }

    Node *newNode = NULL;
    newNode = (Node*)malloc(sizeof(Node));
    strcpy(newNode->data, data);
    newNode->next = p->next; // newNode next point to next node
    p->next = newNode; // current next point to newNode
    newNode->prev = p;
    newNode->next->prev = newNode;
}

void output(Node *node)
{
    Node *p = node;
    Node *end = NULL;
    while (p != NULL)
    {
        printf("%s -> ", p->data);
        end = p;
        p = p->next;
    }
    printf("End\n");

    p = end;
    while (p != NULL)
    {
        printf("%s -> ", p->data);
        p = p->prev;
    }
    printf("Start\n\n");
}
```

```
void freeMemery()
{
   Node *p = head;
   Node *temp = p;

   while (p != NULL)
   {
      temp = p;
      p = p->next;
      free(temp);
   }
}

int main()
{
   init();

   printf("Insert a new node Walnut at index 2 : \n");
   insert(2, "Walnut");

   output(head);
   freeMemery();

   return 0;
}
```

Result:

San Francisco -> Oakland -> Walnut -> Berkeley -> Fremont -> End
Fremont -> Berkeley -> Walnut -> Oakland -> San Francisco -> Start

4. Delete the index=2 node.

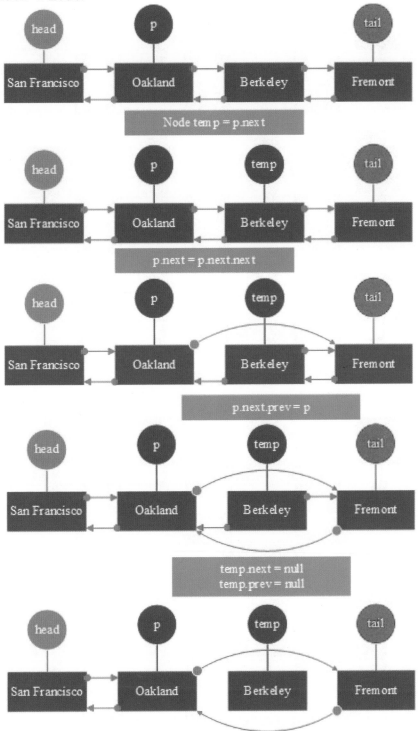

TestDoubleLink.c

```c
#include <stdio.h>
#include<stdlib.h>
#include <string.h>
typedef struct Node
{
    char data[50];
    struct Node *prev;
    struct Node *next;
} Node;

Node *head  = NULL;
Node *tail = NULL;

void init()
{
    head = (Node*)malloc(sizeof(Node));
    strcpy(head->data, "San Francisco");
    head->prev = NULL;
    head->next = NULL;

    Node *nodeOakland = NULL;
    nodeOakland = (Node*)malloc(sizeof(Node));
    strcpy(nodeOakland->data, "Oakland");
    nodeOakland->prev = head;
    nodeOakland->next = NULL;
    head->next = nodeOakland;

    Node *nodeBerkeley = NULL;
    nodeBerkeley = (Node*)malloc(sizeof(Node));
    strcpy(nodeBerkeley->data, "Berkeley");
    nodeBerkeley->prev = nodeOakland;
    nodeBerkeley->next = NULL;
    nodeOakland->next = nodeBerkeley;

    tail = (Node*)malloc(sizeof(Node));
    strcpy(tail->data, "Fremont");
    tail->prev = nodeBerkeley;
    tail->next = NULL;
    nodeBerkeley->next = tail;
}
```

```c
void removeNode(int removePosition)
{
    Node *p = head;
    int i = 0;
    // Move the node to the previous node position that was deleted
    while (p->next != NULL && i < removePosition - 1)
    {
        p = p->next;
        i++;
    }

    Node *temp = p->next;// Save the node you want to delete
    p->next = p->next->next;// Previous node next points to next of delete the node
    p->next->prev = p;
    temp->next = NULL;// Set the delete node next to null
    temp->prev = NULL;// Set the delete node prev to null
    free(temp);
}

void output(Node *node)
{
    Node *p = node;
    Node *end = NULL;
    while (p != NULL)
    {
        printf("%s -> ", p->data);
        end = p;
        p = p->next;
    }
    printf("End\n");

    p = end;
    while (p != NULL)
    {
        printf("%s -> ", p->data);
        p = p->prev;
    }
    printf("Start\n\n");
}
```

```
void freeMemery()
{
    Node *p = head;
    Node *temp = p;

    while (p != NULL)
    {
        temp = p;
        p = p->next;
        free(temp);
    }
}

int main()
{
    init();

    printf("Delete a new node Berkeley at index = 2 : \n");
    removeNode(2);

    output(head);
    freeMemery();

    return 0;
}
```

Result:

San Francisco -> Oakland -> Fremont -> End
Fremont -> Oakland -> San Francisco -> Start

One-way Circular LinkedList

One-way Circular List:

It is a chain storage structure of a linear table, which is connected to form a ring, and each node is composed of data and a pointer to next.

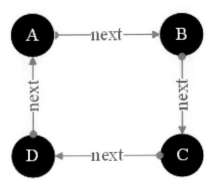

UML Diagram

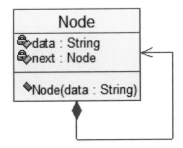

```
typedef struct Node
{
    char data[50];
    struct Node *next;
} Node;
```

1. One-way Circular Linked List initialization and traversal output.

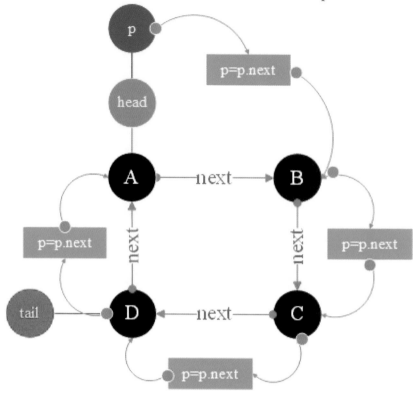

TestSingleCircleLink.c

```c
#include <stdio.h>
#include<stdlib.h>
#include <string.h>

typedef struct Node
{
    char data[50];
    struct Node *next;
} Node;

Node *head  = NULL;
Node *tail = NULL;

void init()
{
    head = (Node*)malloc(sizeof(Node));
    strcpy(head->data, "A");
    head->next = NULL;

    Node *nodeB = NULL;
    nodeB = (Node*)malloc(sizeof(Node));
    strcpy(nodeB->data, "B");
    nodeB->next = NULL;
    head->next = nodeB;

    Node *nodeC = NULL;
    nodeC = (Node*)malloc(sizeof(Node));
    strcpy(nodeC->data, "C");
    nodeC->next = NULL;
    nodeB->next = nodeC;

    tail = (Node*)malloc(sizeof(Node));
    strcpy(tail->data, "D");
    tail->next = head;
    nodeC->next = tail;
}
```

```c
void output(Node *node)
{
    Node *p = node;
    do
    {
        printf("%s -> ", p->data);
        p = p->next;
    } while (p != head);

    printf("%s \n\n", p->data);
}

void freeMemery()
{
    Node *p = head;
    Node *temp = p;

    do
    {
        temp = p;
        p = p->next;
        free(temp);
    } while (p != head);
}

int main()
{
    init();

    output(head);
    freeMemery();

    return 0;
}
```

Result:

A -> B -> C -> D -> A

3. Insert a node E in position 2.

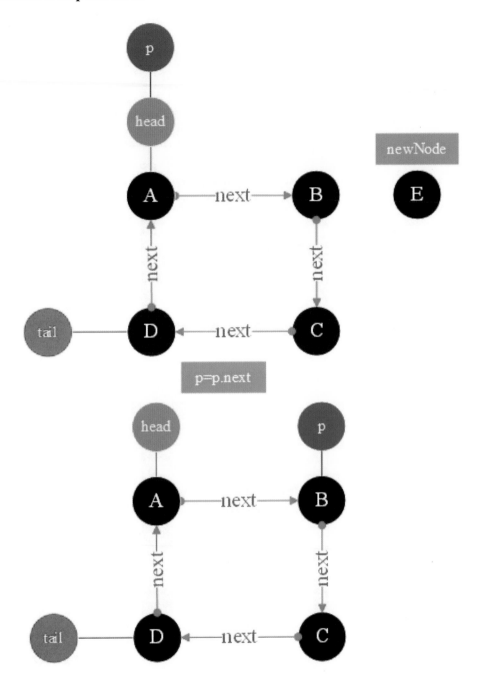

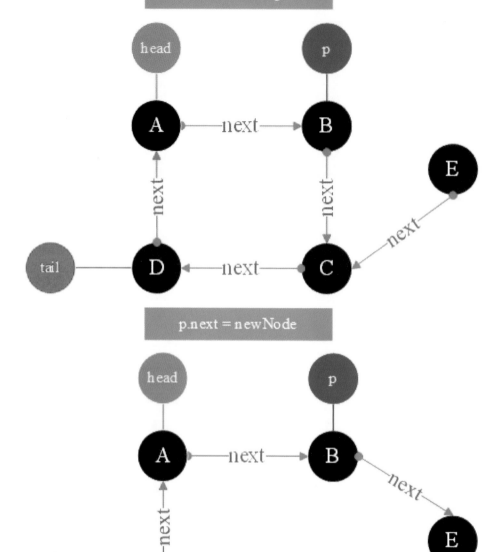

TestSingleCircleLink.c

```c
#include <stdio.h>
#include<stdlib.h>
#include <string.h>

typedef struct Node
{
    char data[50];
    struct Node *next;
} Node;

Node *head  = NULL;
Node *tail = NULL;

void init()
{
    head = (Node*)malloc(sizeof(Node));
    strcpy(head->data, "A");
    head->next = NULL;

    Node *nodeB = NULL;
    nodeB = (Node*)malloc(sizeof(Node));
    strcpy(nodeB->data, "B");
    nodeB->next = NULL;
    head->next = nodeB;

    Node *nodeC = NULL;
    nodeC = (Node*)malloc(sizeof(Node));
    strcpy(nodeC->data, "C");
    nodeC->next = NULL;
    nodeB->next = nodeC;

    tail = (Node*)malloc(sizeof(Node));
    strcpy(tail->data, "D");
    tail->next = head;
    nodeC->next = tail;
}
```

```c
void insert(int insertPosition, char data[])
{
    Node *p = head;
    int i = 0;
    // Move the node to the insertion position
    while (p->next != NULL && i < insertPosition - 1)
    {
        p = p->next;
        i++;
    }

    Node *newNode = NULL;
    newNode = (Node*)malloc(sizeof(Node));
    strcpy(newNode->data, data);
    newNode->next = p->next; // newNode next point to next node
    p->next = newNode; // current next point to newNode
}

void output(Node *node)
{
    Node *p = node;
    do
    {
        printf("%s -> ", p->data);
        p = p->next;
    } while (p != head);

    printf("%s \n\n", p->data);
}

void freeMemery()
{
    Node *p = head;
    Node *temp = p;

    do
    {
        temp = p;
        p = p->next;
        free(temp);
    } while (p != head);
}
```

```
int main()
{
    init();

    printf("Insert a new node E at index = 2 : \n");
    insert(2, "E");

    output(head);
    freeMemery();
    return 0;
}
```

Result:

A -> B -> E -> C -> D -> A

4. Delete the index=2 node.

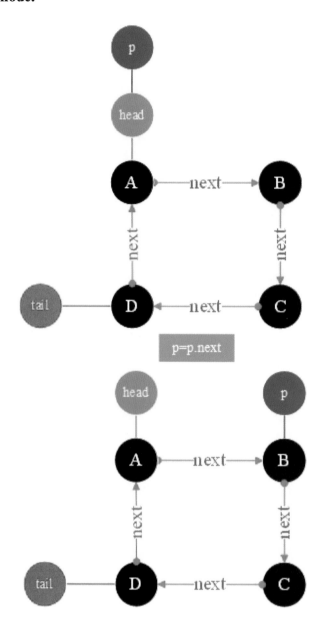

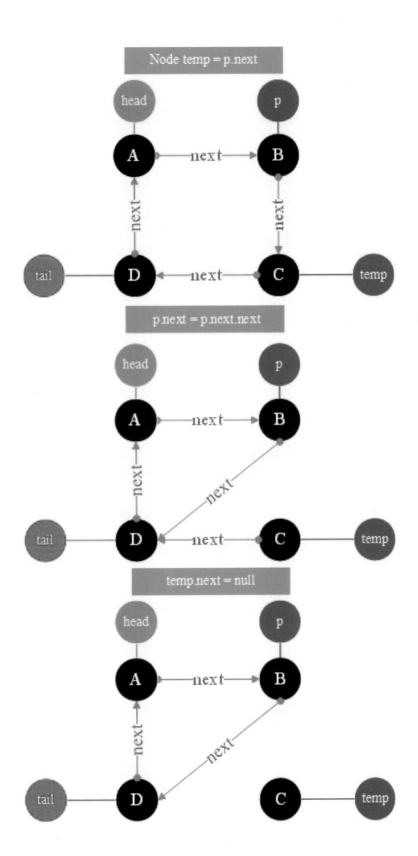

TestSingleCircleLink.c

```c
#include <stdio.h>
#include<stdlib.h>
#include <string.h>

typedef struct Node
{
   char data[50];
   struct Node *next;
} Node;

Node *head  = NULL;
Node *tail = NULL;

void init()
{
   head = (Node*)malloc(sizeof(Node));
   strcpy(head->data, "A");
   head->next = NULL;

   Node *nodeB = NULL;
   nodeB = (Node*)malloc(sizeof(Node));
   strcpy(nodeB->data, "B");
   nodeB->next = NULL;
   head->next = nodeB;

   Node *nodeC = NULL;
   nodeC = (Node*)malloc(sizeof(Node));
   strcpy(nodeC->data, "C");
   nodeC->next = NULL;
   nodeB->next = nodeC;

   tail = (Node*)malloc(sizeof(Node));
   strcpy(tail->data, "D");
   tail->next = head;
   nodeC->next = tail;
}
```

```c
void removeNode(int removePosition)
{
    Node *p = head;
    int i = 0;
    // Move the node to the previous node position that was deleted
    while (p->next != NULL && i < removePosition - 1)
    {
        p = p->next;
        i++;
    }

    Node *temp = p->next;// Save the node you want to delete
    p->next = p->next->next;// Previous node next points to next of delete the node
    temp->next = NULL;
    free(temp);

}

void output(Node *node)
{
    Node *p = node;
    do
    {
        printf("%s -> ", p->data);
        p = p->next;
    } while (p != head);

    printf("%s \n\n", p->data);
}

void freeMemery()
{
    Node *p = head;
    Node *temp = p;

    do
    {
        temp = p;
        p = p->next;
        free(temp);
    } while (p != head);
}
```

```
int main()
{
    init();

    printf("Delete a new node E at index = 2 : \n");
    removeNode(2);

    output(head);
    freeMemery();
    return 0;
}
```

Result:

A -> B -> D -> A

Two-way Circular LinkedList

Two-way Circular List:

It is a chain storage structure of a linear table. The nodes are connected in series by two directions, and is connected to form a ring. Each node is composed of data, pointing to the previous node prev and pointing to the next node next.

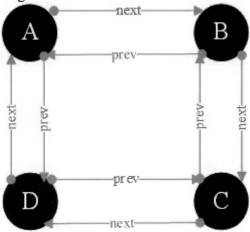

UML Diagram

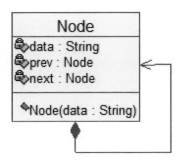

```
typedef struct Node
{
    char data[50];
    struct Node *prev;
    struct Node *next;
} Node;
```

1. Two-way Circular Linked List initialization and traversal output.

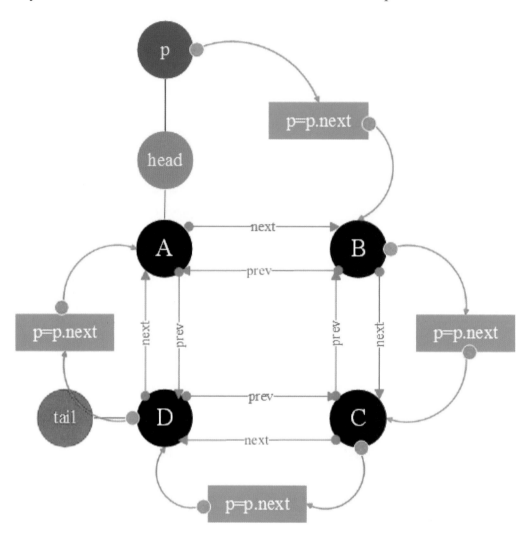

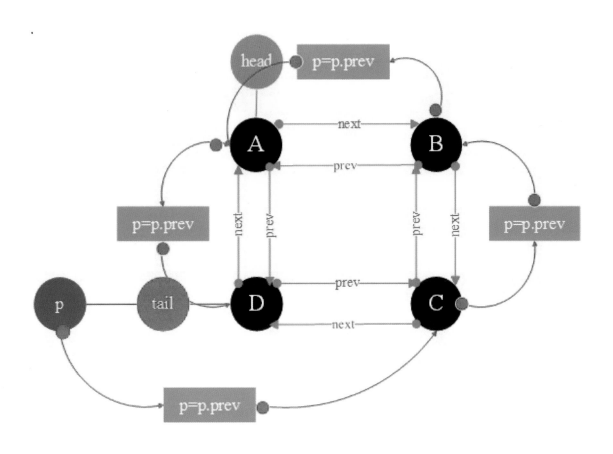

TestDoubleCircleLink.c

```c
#include <stdio.h>
#include<stdlib.h>
#include <string.h>
typedef struct Node
{
    char data[50];
    struct Node *prev;
    struct Node *next;
} Node;

Node *head = NULL;
Node *tail = NULL;

void init()
{
    head = (Node*)malloc(sizeof(Node));
    strcpy(head->data, "A");
    head->prev = NULL;
    head->next = NULL;

    Node *nodeB = NULL;
    nodeB = (Node*)malloc(sizeof(Node));
    strcpy(nodeB->data, "B");
    nodeB->prev = head;
    nodeB->next = NULL;
    head->next = nodeB;

    Node *nodeC = NULL;
    nodeC = (Node*)malloc(sizeof(Node));
    strcpy(nodeC->data, "C");
    nodeC->next = NULL;
    nodeC->prev = nodeB;
    nodeB->next = nodeC;

    tail = (Node*)malloc(sizeof(Node));
    strcpy(tail->data, "D");
    tail->next = head;
    tail->prev = nodeC;
    nodeC->next = tail;
    head->prev = tail;
}
```

```c
void output()
{
    Node *p = head;
    do
    {
        printf("%s -> ", p->data);
        p = p->next;
    } while (p != head);
    printf("%s ", p->data);
    printf("End\n");

    p = tail;
    do
    {
        printf("%s -> ", p->data);
        p = p->prev;
    } while (p != tail);
    printf("%s ", p->data);
    printf("Start\n\n");
}

void freeMemery()
{
    Node *p = head;
    Node *temp = p;
    do
    {
        temp = p;
        p = p->next;
        free(temp);
    } while (p != head);
}

int main()
{
    init();
    output();
    freeMemery();
    return 0;
}
```

Result:
A -> B -> C -> D -> A
D -> C -> B -> A -> D

3. Insert a node E in position 2.

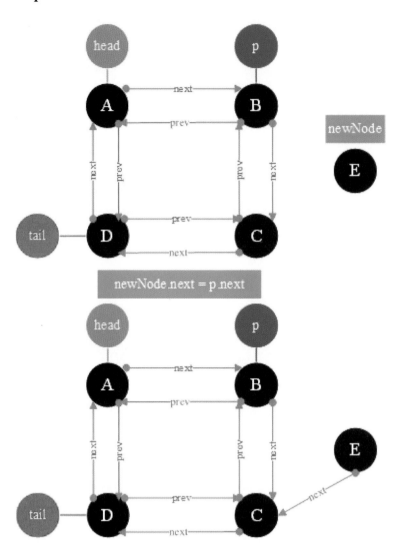

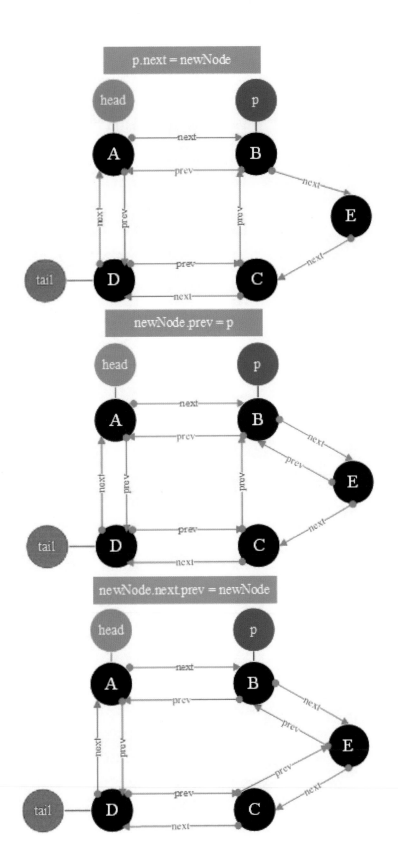

TestDoubleCircleLink.c

```c
#include <stdio.h>
#include<stdlib.h>
#include <string.h>
typedef struct Node
{
    char data[50];
    struct Node *prev;
    struct Node *next;
} Node;

Node *head = NULL;
Node *tail = NULL;

void init()
{
    head = (Node*)malloc(sizeof(Node));
    strcpy(head->data, "A");
    head->prev = NULL;
    head->next = NULL;

    Node *nodeB = NULL;
    nodeB = (Node*)malloc(sizeof(Node));
    strcpy(nodeB->data, "B");
    nodeB->prev = head;
    nodeB->next = NULL;
    head->next = nodeB;

    Node *nodeC = NULL;
    nodeC = (Node*)malloc(sizeof(Node));
    strcpy(nodeC->data, "C");
    nodeC->next = NULL;
    nodeC->prev = nodeB;
    nodeB->next = nodeC;

    tail = (Node*)malloc(sizeof(Node));
    strcpy(tail->data, "D");
    tail->next = head;
    tail->prev = nodeC;
    nodeC->next = tail;
    head->prev = tail;
}
```

```c
void insert(int insertPosition, char data[])
{
    Node *p = head;
    int i = 0;
    // Move the node to the insertion position
    while (p->next != NULL && i < insertPosition - 1)
    {
        p = p->next;
        i++;
    }

    Node *newNode = NULL;
    newNode = (Node*)malloc(sizeof(Node));
    strcpy(newNode->data, data);
    newNode->next = p->next; // newNode next point to next node
    p->next = newNode; // current next point to newNode
    newNode->prev = p;
    newNode->next->prev = newNode;
}

void output()
{
    Node *p = head;
    do
    {
        printf("%s -> ", p->data);
        p = p->next;
    } while (p != head);
    printf("%s ", p->data);
    printf("End\n");

    p = tail;
    do
    {
        printf("%s -> ", p->data);
        p = p->prev;
    } while (p != tail);
    printf("%s ", p->data);
    printf("Start\n\n");
}
```

```
void freeMemery()
{
    Node *p = head;
    Node *temp = p;

    do
    {
        temp = p;
        p = p->next;
        free(temp);
    } while (p != head);
}

int main()
{
    init();

    printf("Insert a new node E at index 2 : \n");
    insert(2, "E");

    output();
    freeMemery();

    return 0;
}
```

Result:

A -> B -> E -> C -> D -> A

D -> C -> E -> B -> A -> D

4. Delete the index=2 node.

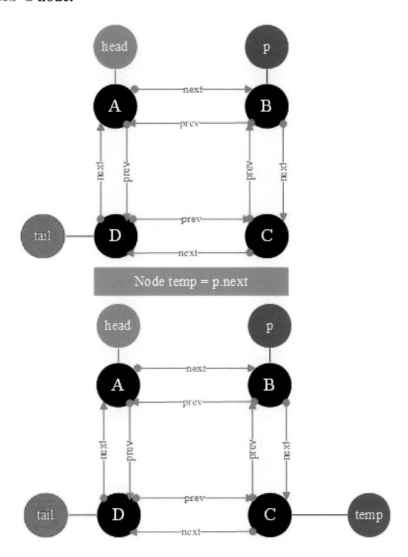

Node temp = p.next

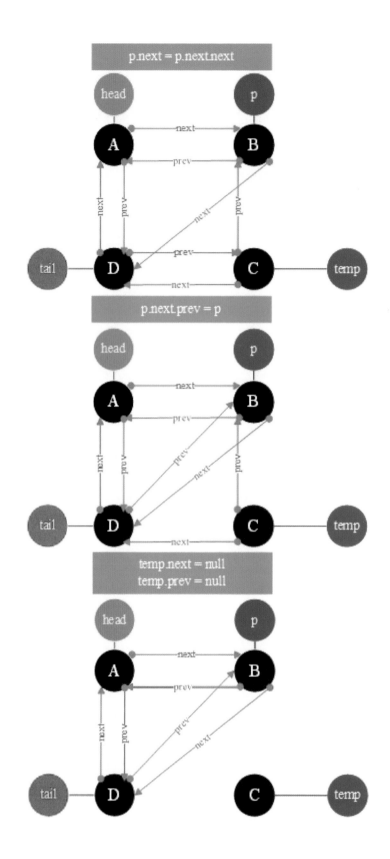

TestDoubleCircleLink.c

```c
#include <stdio.h>
#include<stdlib.h>
#include <string.h>
typedef struct Node
{
    char data[50];
    struct Node *prev;
    struct Node *next;
} Node;

Node *head  = NULL;
Node *tail = NULL;

void init()
{
    head = (Node*)malloc(sizeof(Node));
    strcpy(head->data, "A");
    head->prev = NULL;
    head->next = NULL;

    Node *nodeB = NULL;
    nodeB = (Node*)malloc(sizeof(Node));
    strcpy(nodeB->data, "B");
    nodeB->prev = head;
    nodeB->next = NULL;
    head->next = nodeB;

    Node *nodeC = NULL;
    nodeC = (Node*)malloc(sizeof(Node));
    strcpy(nodeC->data, "C");
    nodeC->next = NULL;
    nodeC->prev = nodeB;
    nodeB->next = nodeC;

    tail = (Node*)malloc(sizeof(Node));
    strcpy(tail->data, "D");
    tail->next = head;
    tail->prev = nodeC;
    nodeC->next = tail;
    head->prev = tail;
}
```

```c
void removeNode(int removePosition)
{
    Node *p = head;
    int i = 0;
    // Move the node to the previous node position that was deleted
    while (p->next != NULL && i < removePosition - 1)
    {
        p = p->next;
        i++;
    }

    Node *temp = p->next;// Save the node you want to delete
    p->next = p->next->next;// Previous node next points to next of delete the node
    p->next->prev = p;
    temp->next = NULL;// Set the delete node next to null
    temp->prev = NULL;// Set the delete node prev to null
    free(temp);
}

void output()
{
    Node *p = head;
    do
    {
        printf("%s -> ", p->data);
        p = p->next;
    } while (p != head);
    printf("%s ", p->data);
    printf("End\n");

    p = tail;
    do
    {
        printf("%s -> ", p->data);
        p = p->prev;
    } while (p != tail);
    printf("%s ", p->data);
    printf("Start\n\n");
}
```

```
void freeMemery()
{
    Node *p = head;
    Node *temp = p;

    do
    {
        temp = p;
        p = p->next;
        free(temp);
    } while (p != head);
}

int main()
{
    init();

    printf("Delete a new node C at index = 2 : \n");
    removeNode(2);

    output();
    freeMemery();

    return 0;
}
```

Result:

A -> B -> D -> A

D -> B -> A -> D

Queue

Queue:
FIFO (First In First Out) sequence.

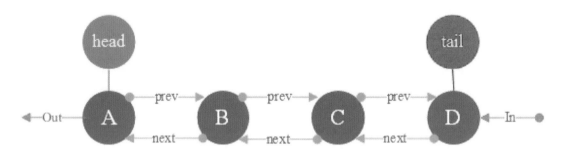

UML Diagram

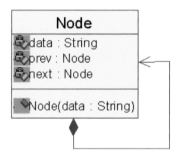

```
typedef struct Node
{
    char data[50];
    struct Node *prev;
    struct Node *next;
} Node;
```

1. Queue initialization and traversal output.

Initialization Insert A

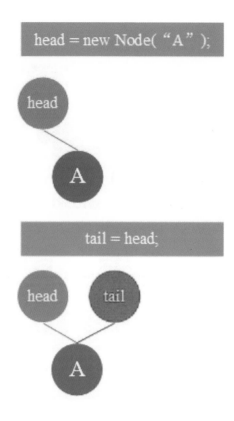

Initialization Insert B

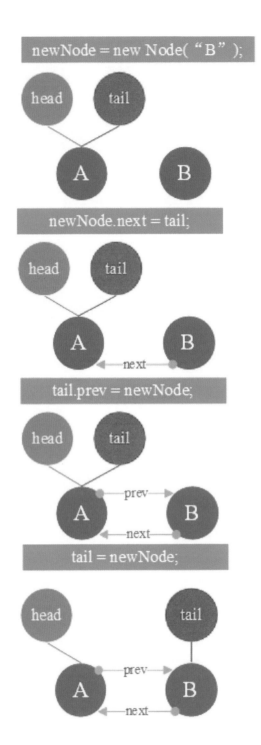

Initialization Insert C

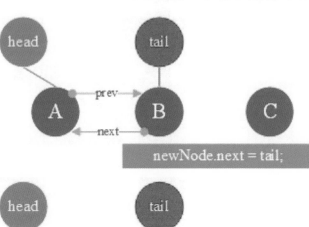

newNode = new Node("C");

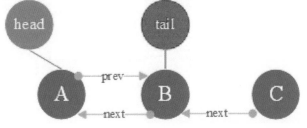

newNode.next = tail;

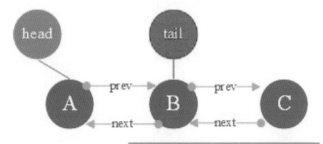

tail.prev = newNode;

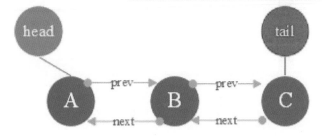

tail = newNode;

Initialization Insert D

newNode = new Node("D");

newNode.next = tail;

tail.prev = newNode;

tail = newNode;

108

Queue.c

```c
#include <stdio.h>
#include<stdlib.h>
#include <string.h>

typedef struct Node
{
    char data[50];
    struct Node *prev;
    struct Node *next;
} Node;

Node *head  = NULL;
Node *tail = NULL;
int size;

void offer(char element[])
{
    if (head == NULL)
    {
        head = (Node*)malloc(sizeof(Node));
        strcpy(head->data, element);
        tail = head;
    }
    else
    {
        Node *newNode = NULL;
        newNode = (Node*)malloc(sizeof(Node));
        strcpy(newNode->data, element);
        newNode->next = tail;
        tail->prev = newNode;
        tail = newNode;
    }
    size++;
}
```

```c
Node *poll()
{
    Node *p = head;

    if (p == NULL)
    {
        return NULL;
    }

    head = head->prev;

    p->next = NULL;
    p->prev = NULL;

    size--;
    return p;
}

void output()
{
    Node *p = head;

    printf("Head ");
    Node *node = NULL;
    while ((node = poll())!=NULL) {
        printf("%s <- ", node->data);
    }
    printf("Tail\n");
}

void freeMemery()
{
    Node *p = head;
    Node *temp = p;

    while (p != NULL)
    {
        temp = p;
        p = p->next;
        free(temp);
    }
}
```

```
int main()
{
    offer("A");
    offer("B");
    offer("C");
    offer("D");

    output();

    freeMemery();

    return 0;
}
```

Result:

Head A <- B <- C <- D <- Tail

Stack

Stack:
FILO (First In Last Out) sequence.

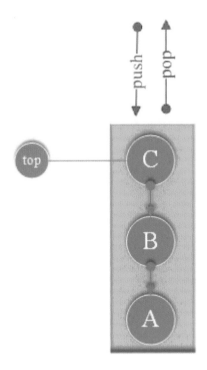

UML Diagram

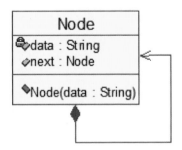

```
typedef struct Node
{
    char data[50];
    struct Node *next;
} Node;
```

1. Stack initialization and traversal output.

Push A into Stack

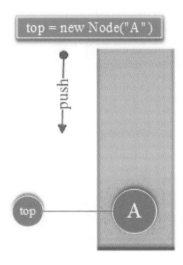

Push B into Stack

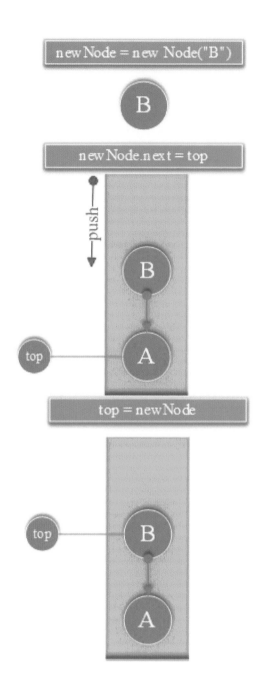

Push C into Stack

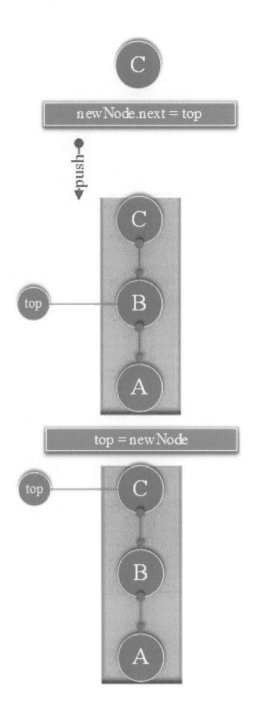

If pop C from Stack:

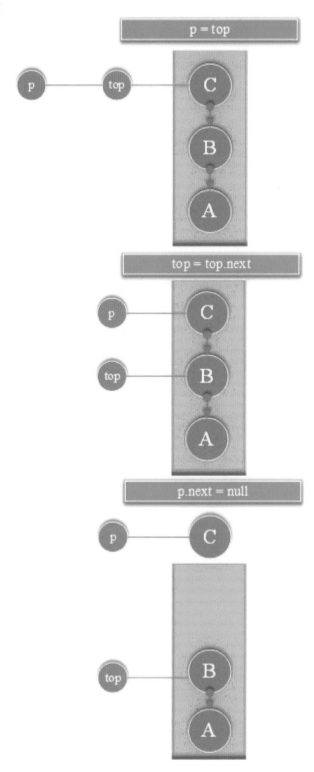

If pop B from Stack:

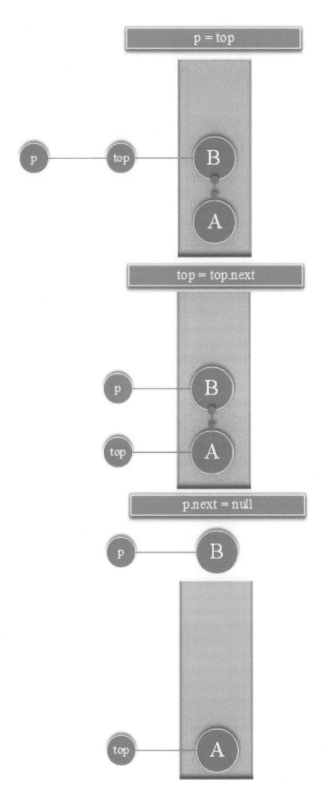

If pop A from Stack:

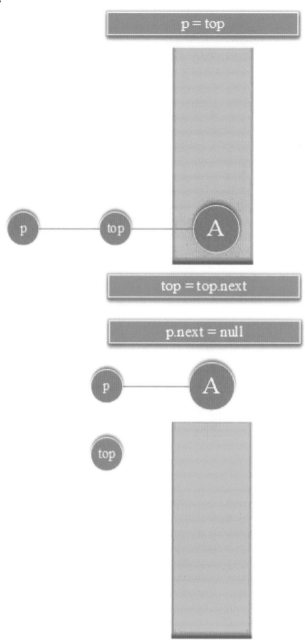

Stack.c

```c
#include <stdio.h>
#include<stdlib.h>
#include <string.h>
typedef struct Node
{
    char data[50];
    struct Node *prev;
    struct Node *next;
} Node;

Node *top = NULL;
int size;

void push(char element[])
{
    if (top == NULL)
    {
        top = (Node*)malloc(sizeof(Node));
        strcpy(top->data, element);
    }
    else
    {
        Node *newNode = NULL;
        newNode = (Node*)malloc(sizeof(Node));
        strcpy(newNode->data, element);
        newNode->next = top;
        top = newNode;
    }
    size++;
}

Node *pop()
{
    if (top == NULL)
    {
        return NULL;
    }
    Node *p = top;
    top = top->next;// top move down
    p->next = NULL;
    size--;
    return p;
}
```

```c
void output()
{
    printf("Top ");
    Node *node = NULL;
    while ((node = pop())!=NULL) {
        printf("%s -> ", node->data);
    }
    printf("End\n");
}

void freeMemery()
{
    Node *p = top;
    Node *temp = p;

    while (p != NULL)
    {
        temp = p;
        p = p->next;
        free(temp);
    }
}

int main()
{
    push("A");
    push("B");
    push("C");
    push("D");

    output();

    freeMemery();
    return 0;
}
```

Result:

Top D -> C -> B -> A -> End

Recursive Algorithm

Recursive Algorithm:
The program function itself calls its own layer to progress until it reaches a certain condition and step by step returns to the end..

1. Factorial of n : n*(n-1)*(n-2) *2*1

TestFactorial.c

```c
#include <stdio.h>

long factorial(int n)
{
    if (n == 1)
    {
        return 1;
    }
    else
    {
        return factorial(n - 1) * n;//Recursively call yourself until the end of the return
    }
}

int main()
{
    int n = 5;
    long fac = factorial(n);
    printf("The factorial of 5 is : %ld", fac);

    return 0;
}
```

Result:

The factorial of 5 is :120

Graphical analysis:

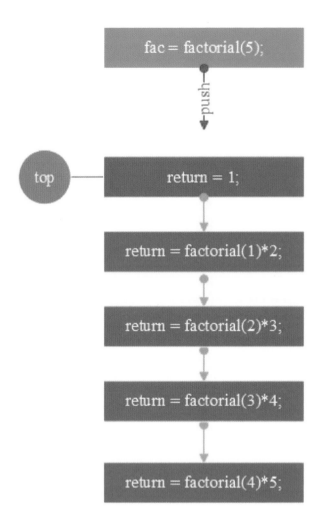

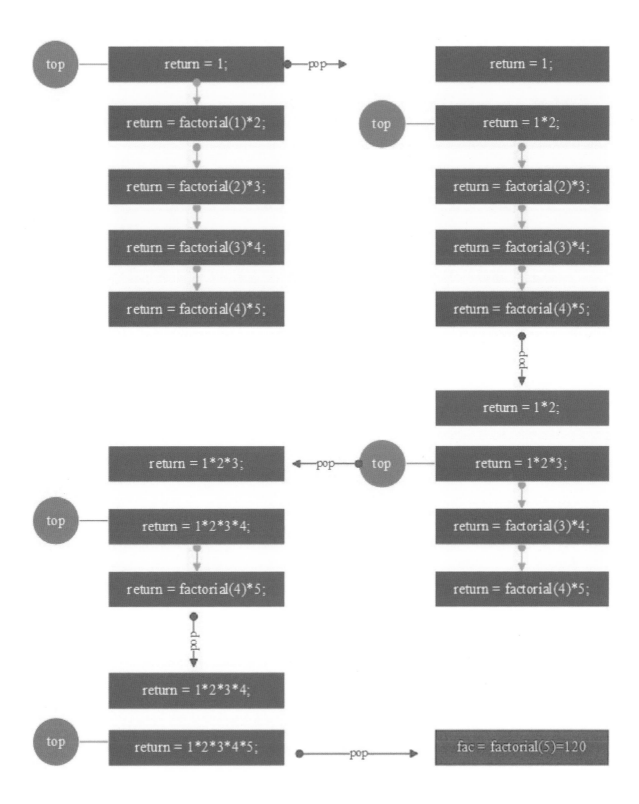

Two-way Merge Algorithm

Two-way Merge Algorithm:
The data of the first half and the second half are sorted, and the two ordered sub-list are merged into one ordered list, which continue to recursive to the end.

1. The scores {50, 65, 99, 87, 74, 63, 76, 100} by merge sort

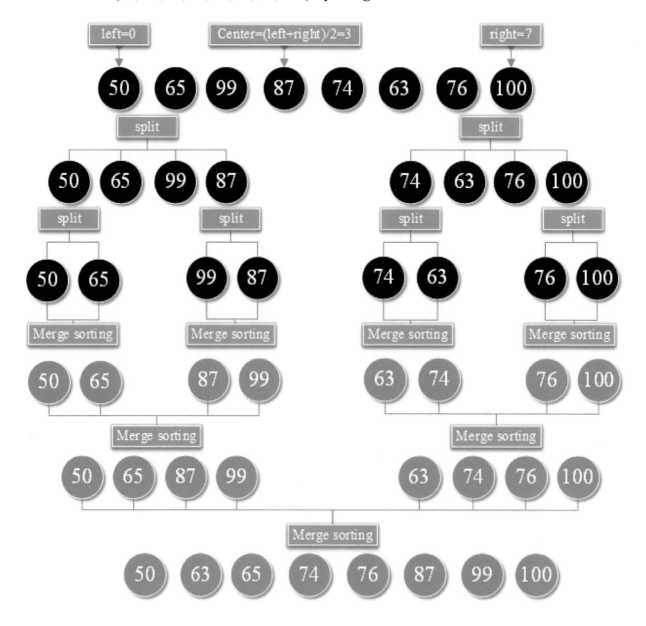

TestMergeSort.c

```c
#include <stdio.h>

void sort(int array[], int length) ;
void mergeSort(int array[], int temp[], int left, int right) ;
void merge(int array[], int temp[], int left, int right, int rightEndIndex) ;

int main()
{
    int scores[] = { 50, 65, 99, 87, 74, 63, 76, 100, 92 };
    int length = sizeof(scores) / sizeof(scores[0]);

    sort(scores, length);

    int i;
    for (i = 0; i < length; i++)
    {
        printf("%d,", scores[i]);
    }

    return 0;
}

void sort(int array[], int length)
{
    int temp[length];
    mergeSort(array, temp, 0, length - 1);
}

void mergeSort(int array[], int temp[], int left, int right)
{
    if (left < right)
    {
        int center = (left + right) / 2;
        mergeSort(array, temp, left, center); // Left merge sort
        mergeSort(array, temp, center + 1, right); // Right merge sort
        merge(array, temp, left, center + 1, right); // Merge two ordered arrays
    }
}
```

```
/**
 Combine two ordered list into an ordered list
 temp : Temporary array
 left :    Start the subscript on the left
 right :  Start the subscript on the right
 rightEndIndex : End subscript on the right
 */
void merge(int array[], int temp[], int left, int right, int rightEndIndex)
{
    int leftEndIndex = right - 1; // End subscript on the left
    int tempIndex = left; // Starting from the left count
    int elementNumber = rightEndIndex - left + 1;

    while (left <= leftEndIndex && right <= rightEndIndex)
    {
        if (array[left] <= array[right])
            temp[tempIndex++] = array[left++];
        else
            temp[tempIndex++] = array[right++];
    }

    while (left <= leftEndIndex)
    {
        // If there is element on the left
        temp[tempIndex++] = array[left++];
    }

    while (right <= rightEndIndex)
    {
        // If there is element on the right
        temp[tempIndex++] = array[right++];
    }

    // Copy temp to array
    int i;
    for (i = 0; i < elementNumber; i++)
    {
        array[rightEndIndex] = temp[rightEndIndex];
        rightEndIndex--;
    }
}
```

Result:
50,63,65,74,76,87,92,99,100,

Quick Sort Algorithm

Quick Sort Algorithm:

Quicksort is a popular sorting algorithm that is often faster in practice compared to other sorting algorithms. It utilizes a divide-and-conquer strategy to quickly sort data items by dividing a large array into two smaller arrays.

1. The scores {90, 60, 50, 80, 70, 100} by quick sort

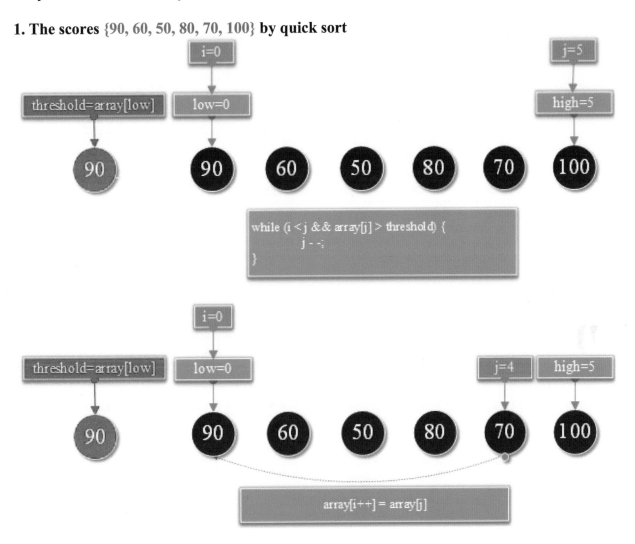

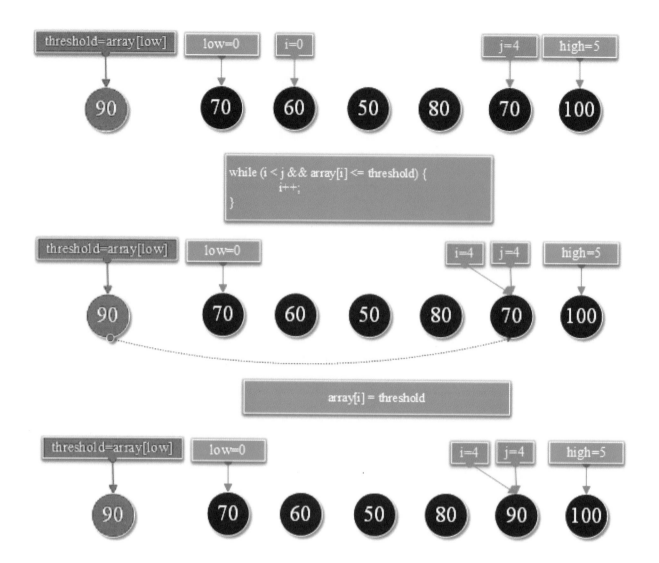

```
while (i < j && array[i] <= threshold) {
        i++;
}
```

array[i] = threshold

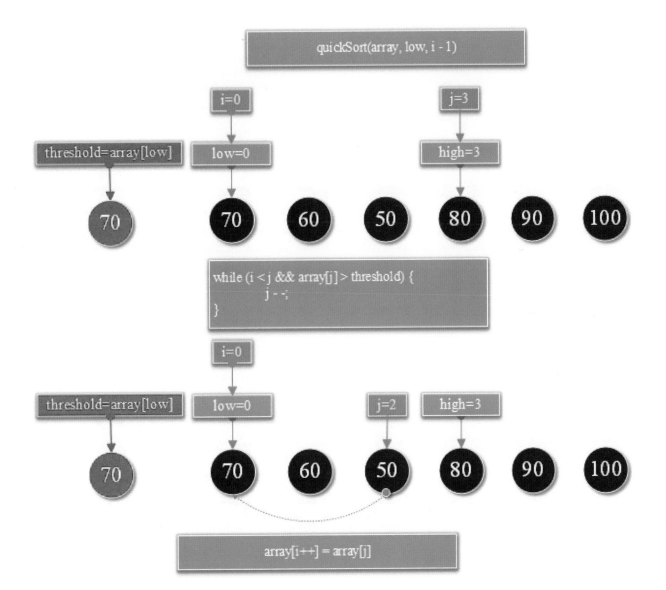

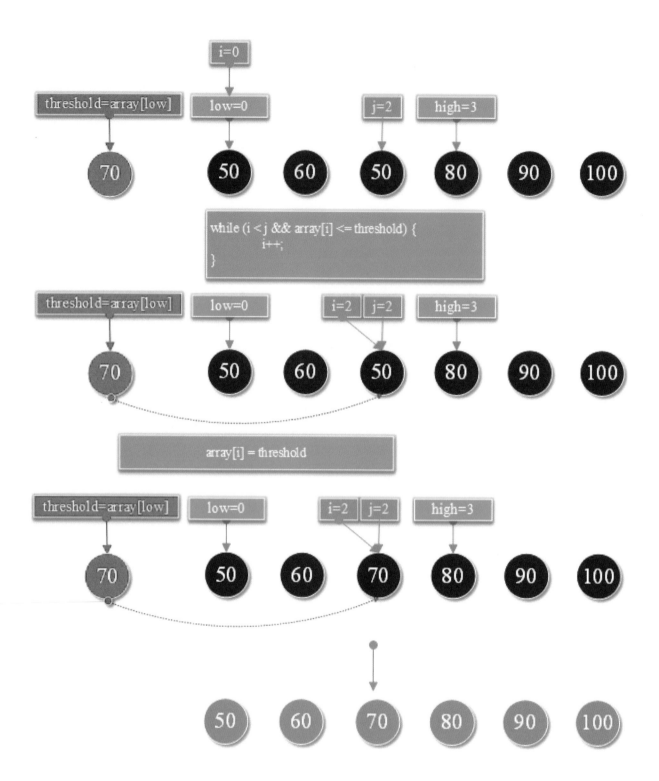

TestQuickSort.c

```c
#include <stdio.h>

void sort(int array[], int length) ;
void quickSort(int array[], int low, int high);

int main()
{
    int scores[] = { 50, 65, 99, 87, 74, 63, 76, 100, 92 };
    int length = sizeof(scores) / sizeof(scores[0]);

    sort(scores, length);

    int i;
    for (i = 0; i < length; i++)
    {
        printf("%d,", scores[i]);
    }

    return 0;
}

void sort(int array[], int length)
{
    if (length > 0)
    {
        quickSort(array, 0, length - 1);
    }
}
```

```
void quickSort(int array[], int low, int high)
{
    if (low > high)
    {
        return;
    }

    int i = low;
    int j = high;
    int threshold = array[low];

    // Alternately scanned from both ends of the list
    while (i < j)
    {
        // Find the first position less than threshold from right to left
        while (i < j && array[j] > threshold)
        {
            j--;
        }
        //Replace the low with a smaller number than the threshold
        if (i < j)
            array[i++] = array[j];

        // Find the first position greater than threshold from left to right
        while (i < j && array[i] <= threshold)
        {
            i++;
        }

        //Replace the high with a number larger than the threshold
        if (i < j)
            array[j--] = array[i];
    }
    array[i] = threshold;
    quickSort (array, low, i - 1); // left quickSort
    quickSort (array, i + 1, high); // right quickSort
}
```

Result:

50,60,70,80,90,100,

Binary Search Tree

Binary Search Tree:
1. If the left subtree of any node is not empty, the value of all nodes on the left subtree is less than the value of its root node;
2. If the right subtree of any node is not empty, the value of all nodes on the right subtree is greater than the value of its root node;
3. The left subtree and the right subtree of any node are also binary search trees.

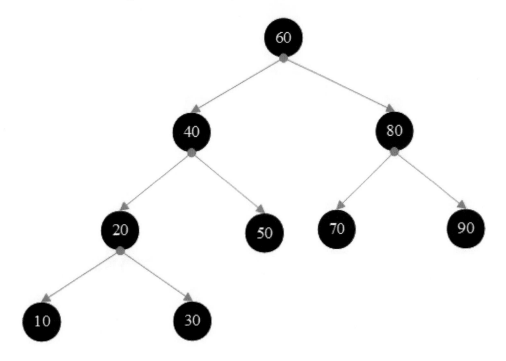

Node UML Diagram

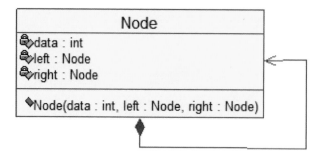

```
typedef struct Node
{
    int data;
    struct Node *left;
    struct Node *right;
} Node;
```

1.Construct a binary search tree, insert node

The inserted nodes are compared from the root node, and the smaller than the root node is compared with the left subtree of the root node, otherwise, compared with the right subtree until the left subtree is empty or the right subtree is empty, then is inserted.

Insert 60

Insert 40

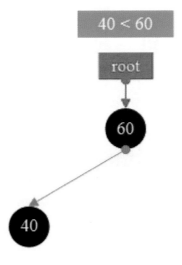

Insert 20

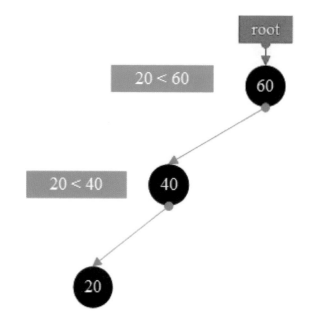

Insert 10

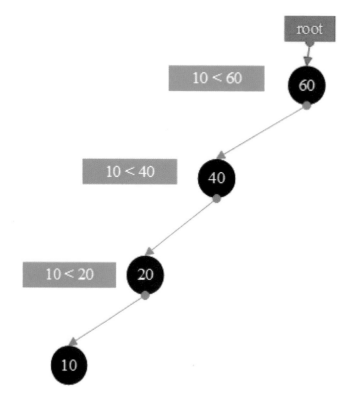

Insert 30

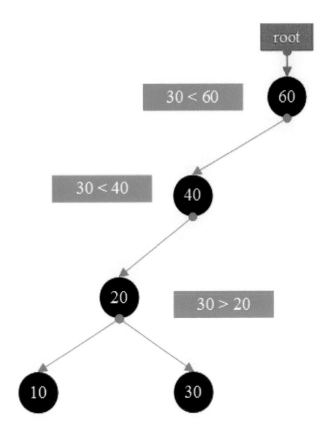

30 < 60

30 < 40

30 > 20

Insert 50

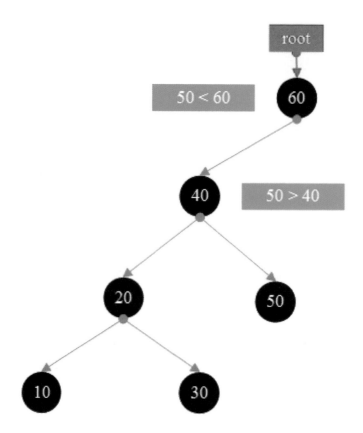

Insert 80

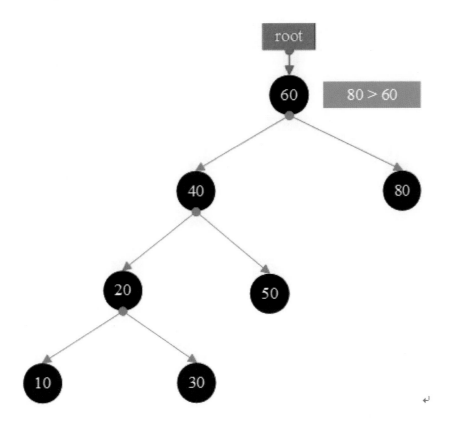

Insert 70

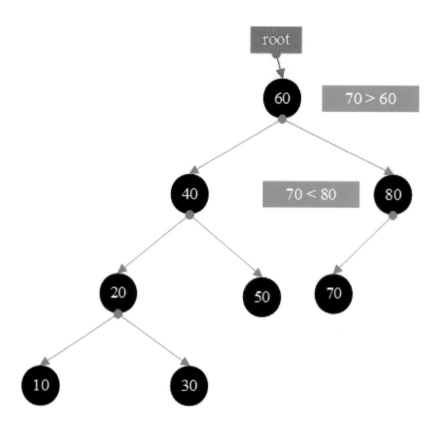

Insert 90

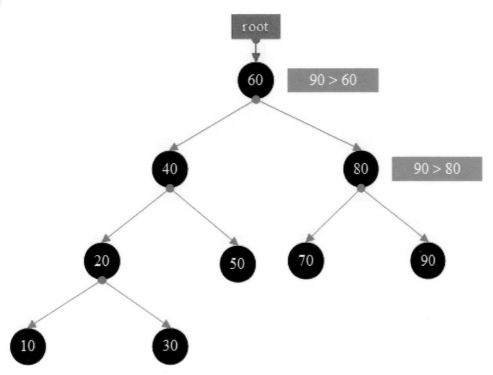

2. binary search tree In-order traversal
In-order traversal : left subtree -> root node -> right subtree

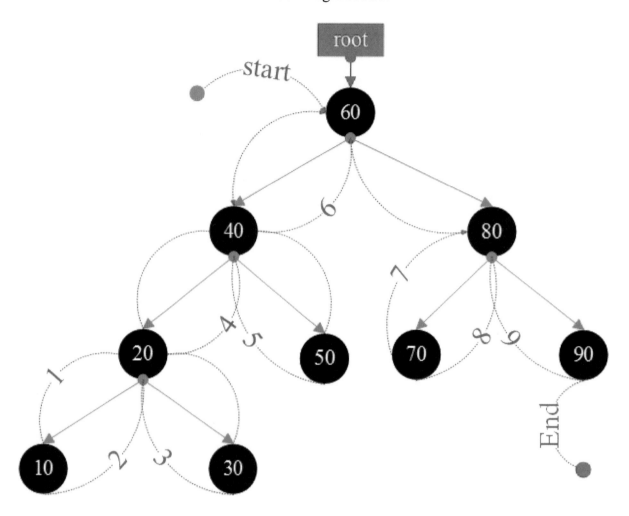

Result:

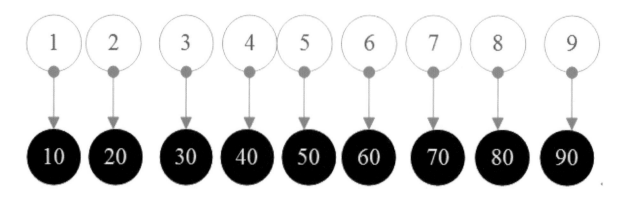

BinaryTree.c

```c
#include <stdio.h>
#include<stdlib.h>

typedef struct Node
{
   int data;
   struct Node *left;
   struct Node *right;

} Node;

Node *root  = NULL;

Node *createNewNode(int newData)
{
   Node *newNode = NULL;
   newNode = (Node*)malloc(sizeof(Node));
   newNode->data = newData;
   newNode->left = NULL;
   newNode->right = NULL;
   return newNode;
}

// In-order traversal binary search tree
void inOrder(Node *root)
{
   if (root == NULL)
   {
      return;
   }
   inOrder(root->left); // Traversing the left subtree
   printf("%d, ", root->data);
   inOrder(root->right); // Traversing the right subtree
}
```

```c
void insert(Node *node, int newData)
{
    if (root == NULL)
    {
        root = (Node*)malloc(sizeof(Node));
        root->data = newData;
        root->left = NULL;
        root->right = NULL;
        return;
    }

    int compareValue = newData - node->data;

    //Recursive left subtree, continue to find the insertion position
    if (compareValue < 0)
    {
        if (node->left == NULL)
        {
            node->left = createNewNode(newData);
        }
        else
        {
            insert(node->left, newData);
        }
    }
    else if (compareValue > 0)
    {
        //Recursive right subtree, continue to find the insertion position
        if (node->right == NULL)
        {

            node->right = createNewNode(newData);
        }
        else
        {
            insert(node->right, newData);
        }
    }
}
```

```c
void freeMemery(Node *node)
{
    if (node == NULL)
    {
        return;
    }
    freeMemery(node->left); // Traversing the left subtree
    freeMemery(node->right); // Traversing the right subtree
    free(node);
}

int main()
{
    //Constructing a binary search tree
    insert(root, 60);
    insert(root, 40);
    insert(root, 20);
    insert(root, 10);
    insert(root, 30);
    insert(root, 50);
    insert(root, 80);
    insert(root, 70);
    insert(root, 90);

    printf("In-order traversal binary search tree \n");
    inOrder(root);

    freeMemery(root);

    return 0;
}
```

Result:

In-order traversal binary search tree
10, 20, 30, 40, 50, 60, 70, 80, 90,

3. binary search tree Pre-order traversal
Pre-order traversal : root node -> left subtree -> right subtree

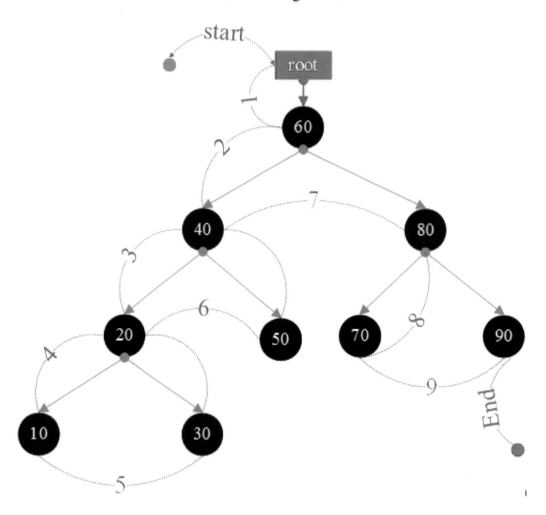

Result:

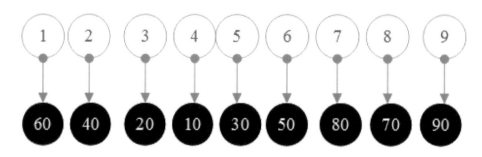

BinaryTree.c

```c
#include <stdio.h>
#include<stdlib.h>

typedef struct Node
{
    int data;
    struct Node *left;
    struct Node *right;

} Node;

Node *root = NULL;

Node *createNewNode(int newData)
{
    Node *newNode = NULL;
    newNode = (Node*)malloc(sizeof(Node));
    newNode->data = newData;
    newNode->left = NULL;
    newNode->right = NULL;
    return newNode;
}

//Preorder traversal binary search tree
void preOrder(Node *root) {
    if (root == NULL) {
        return;
    }
    printf("%d, ", root->data);
    preOrder(root->left); // Recursive Traversing the left subtree
    preOrder(root->right); // Recursive Traversing the right subtree
}
```

```c
void insert(Node *node, int newData)
{
    if (root == NULL)
    {
        root = (Node*)malloc(sizeof(Node));
        root->data = newData;
        root->left = NULL;
        root->right = NULL;
        return;
    }

    int compareValue = newData - node->data;

    //Recursive left subtree, continue to find the insertion position
    if (compareValue < 0)
    {
        if (node->left == NULL)
        {
            node->left = createNewNode(newData);
        }
        else
        {
            insert(node->left, newData);
        }
    }
    else if (compareValue > 0)
    {
        //Recursive right subtree, continue to find the insertion position
        if (node->right == NULL)
        {

            node->right = createNewNode(newData);
        }
        else
        {
            insert(node->right, newData);
        }
    }
}
```

```
void freeMemery(Node *node)
{
    if (node == NULL)
    {
        return;
    }
    freeMemery(node->left); // Traversing the left subtree
    freeMemery(node->right); // Traversing the right subtree
    free(node);
}

int main()
{
    //Constructing a binary search tree
    insert(root, 60);
    insert(root, 40);
    insert(root, 20);
    insert(root, 10);
    insert(root, 30);
    insert(root, 50);
    insert(root, 80);
    insert(root, 70);
    insert(root, 90);

    printf("Pre-order traversal binary search tree \n");
    preOrder(root);

    freeMemery(root);

    return 0;
}
```

Result:

Pre-order traversal binary search tree
60, 40, 20, 10, 30, 50, 80, 70, 90,

4. binary search tree Post-order traversal
Post-order traversal : right subtree -> root node -> left subtree

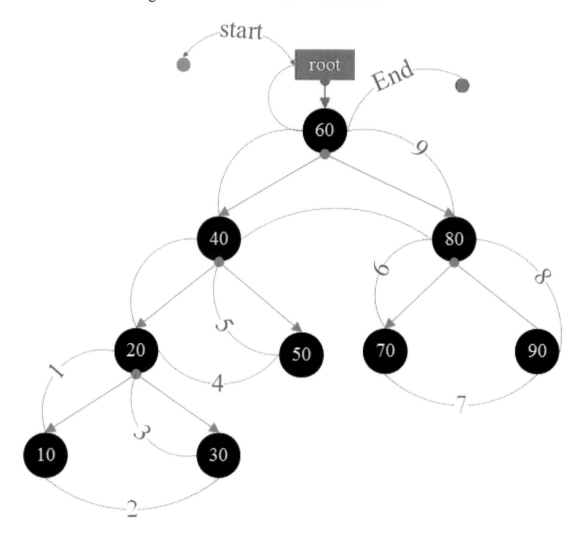

Result:

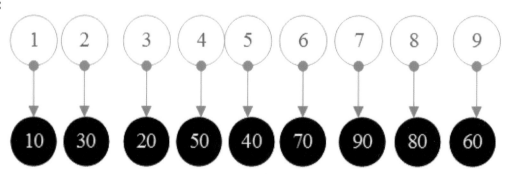

BinaryTree.c

```c
#include <stdio.h>
#include<stdlib.h>

typedef struct Node
{
    int data;
    struct Node *left;
    struct Node *right;

} Node;

Node *root = NULL;

Node *createNewNode(int newData)
{
    Node *newNode = NULL;
    newNode = (Node*)malloc(sizeof(Node));
    newNode->data = newData;
    newNode->left = NULL;
    newNode->right = NULL;
    return newNode;
}

//Post-order traversal binary search tree
void postOrder(Node *root) {
    if (root == NULL) {
        return;
    }

    postOrder(root->left); // Recursive Traversing the left subtree
    postOrder(root->right); // Recursive Traversing the right subtree
    printf("%d, ", root->data);
}
```

```c
void insert(Node *node, int newData)
{
    if (root == NULL)
    {
        root = (Node*)malloc(sizeof(Node));
        root->data = newData;
        root->left = NULL;
        root->right = NULL;
        return;
    }

    int compareValue = newData - node->data;

    //Recursive left subtree, continue to find the insertion position
    if (compareValue < 0)
    {
        if (node->left == NULL)
        {
            node->left = createNewNode(newData);
        }
        else
        {
            insert(node->left, newData);
        }
    }
    else if (compareValue > 0)
    {
        //Recursive right subtree, continue to find the insertion position
        if (node->right == NULL)
        {

            node->right = createNewNode(newData);
        }
        else
        {
            insert(node->right, newData);
        }
    }
}
```

```
void freeMemery(Node *node)
{
    if (node == NULL)
    {
        return;
    }
    freeMemery(node->left); // Traversing the left subtree
    freeMemery(node->right); // Traversing the right subtree
    free(node);
}

int main()
{
    //Constructing a binary search tree
    insert(root, 60);
    insert(root, 40);
    insert(root, 20);
    insert(root, 10);
    insert(root, 30);
    insert(root, 50);
    insert(root, 80);
    insert(root, 70);
    insert(root, 90);

    printf("Post-order traversal binary search tree \n");
    postOrder(root);

    freeMemery(root);

    return 0;
}
```

Result:

Post-order traversal binary search tree
10, 30, 20, 50, 40, 70, 90, 80, 60,

5. binary search tree Maximum and minimum
Minimum value: The small value is on the left child node, as long as the recursion traverses the left child until be empty, the current node is the minimum node.

Maximum value: The large value is on the right child node, as long as the recursive traversal is the right child until be empty, the current node is the largest node.

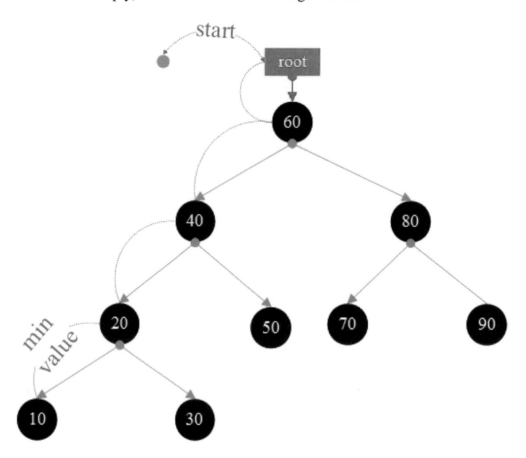

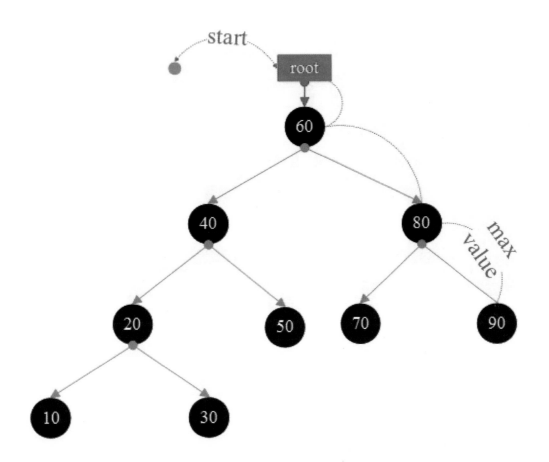

BinaryTree.c

```c
#include <stdio.h>
#include<stdlib.h>
typedef struct Node
{
    int data;
    struct Node *left;
    struct Node *right;
} Node;

Node *root = NULL;

Node *createNewNode(int newData)
{
    Node *newNode = NULL;
    newNode = (Node*)malloc(sizeof(Node));
    newNode->data = newData;
    newNode->left = NULL;
    newNode->right = NULL;
    return newNode;
}

Node *searchMinValue(Node *node) //Minimum value
{
    if (node == NULL || node->data == 0)
        return NULL;
    if (node->left == NULL)
    {
        return node;
    }
    return searchMinValue(node->left);//Recursively find the minimum from the left subtree
}

Node *searchMaxValue(Node *node) //Maximum value
{
    if (node == NULL || node->data == 0)
        return NULL;
    if (node->right == NULL)
    {
        return node;
    }
    return searchMaxValue(node->right);//Recursivelyfind minimum from right subtree
}
```

```c
void insert(Node *node, int newData)
{
    if (root == NULL)
    {
        root = (Node*)malloc(sizeof(Node));
        root->data = newData;
        root->left = NULL;
        root->right = NULL;
        return;
    }

    int compareValue = newData - node->data;

    //Recursive left subtree, continue to find the insertion position
    if (compareValue < 0)
    {
        if (node->left == NULL)
        {
            node->left = createNewNode(newData);
        }
        else
        {
            insert(node->left, newData);
        }
    }
    else if (compareValue > 0)
    {
        //Recursive right subtree, continue to find the insertion position
        if (node->right == NULL)
        {

            node->right = createNewNode(newData);
        }
        else
        {
            insert(node->right, newData);
        }
    }
}
```

```c
void freeMemery(Node *node)
{
    if (node == NULL)
    {
        return;
    }
    freeMemery(node->left); // Traversing the left subtree
    freeMemery(node->right); // Traversing the right subtree
    free(node);
}

int main()
{
    //Constructing a binary search tree
    insert(root, 60);
    insert(root, 40);
    insert(root, 20);
    insert(root, 10);
    insert(root, 30);
    insert(root, 50);
    insert(root, 80);
    insert(root, 70);
    insert(root, 90);

    printf("\nMinimum Value \n");
    Node *minNode = searchMinValue(root);
    printf("%d", minNode->data);

    printf("\nMaximum Value \n");
    Node *maxNode = searchMaxValue(root);
    printf("%d", maxNode->data);

    freeMemery(root);
    return 0;
}
```

Result:
Minimum Value
10

Maximum Value
90

6. binary search tree Delete Node

Binary search tree delete node 3 cases
1. If there is no child node, delete it directly
2. If there is only one child node, the child node replaces the current node, and then deletes the current node.
3. If there are two child nodes, replace the current node with the smallest node from the right subtree, because the smallest node on the right is also larger than the value on the left.

1. If there is no child node, delete it directly: delete node 10

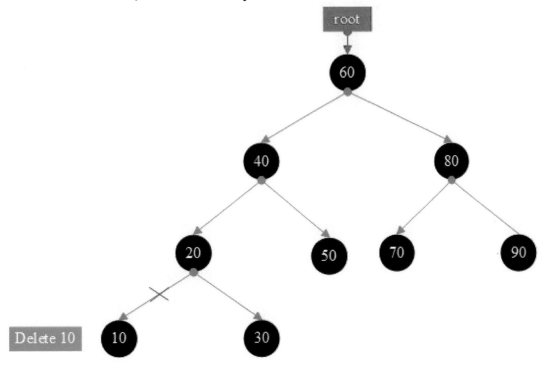

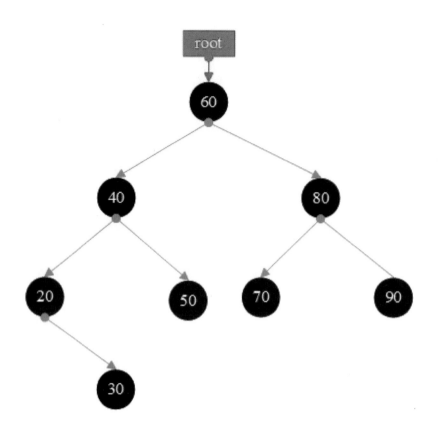

2. If there is only one child node, the child node replaces the current node, and then deletes the current node. Delete node 20

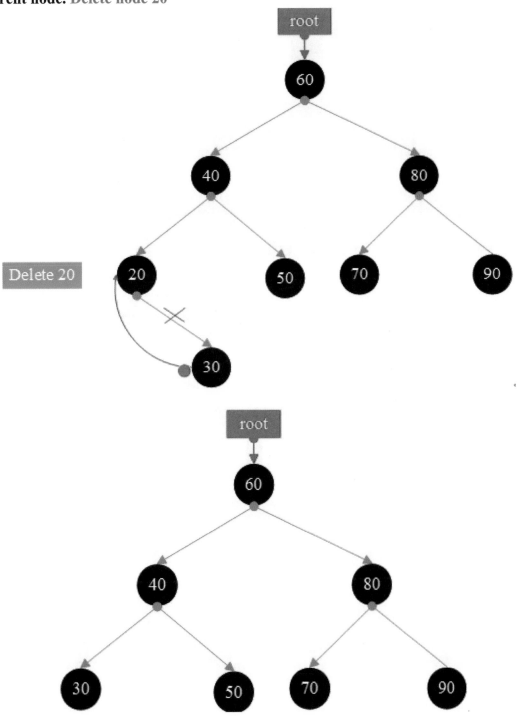

3. If there are two child nodes, replace the current node with the smallest node from the right subtree, Delete node 40

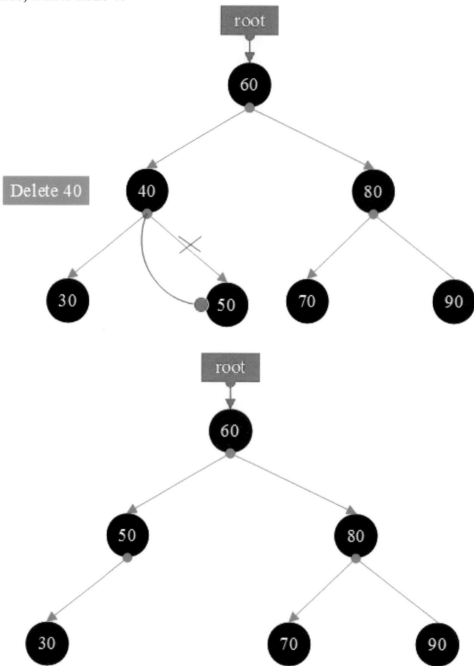

BinaryTree.c

```c
#include <stdio.h>
#include<stdlib.h>
typedef struct Node
{
    int data;
    struct Node *left;
    struct Node *right;
} Node;

Node *root = NULL;

Node *createNewNode(int newData)
{
    Node *newNode = NULL;
    newNode = (Node*)malloc(sizeof(Node));
    newNode->data = newData;
    newNode->left = NULL;
    newNode->right = NULL;
    return newNode;
}

Node *searchMinValue(Node *node) //Minimum value
{
    if (node == NULL || node->data == 0)
        return NULL;
    if (node->left == NULL)
    {
        return node;
    }
    return searchMinValue(node->left);//Recursively find the minimum from the left subtree
}

void inOrder(Node *root)
{
    if (root == NULL)
    {
        return;
    }
    inOrder(root->left); // Traversing the left subtree
    printf("%d, ", root->data);
    inOrder(root->right); // Traversing the right subtree
}
```

```c
Node *removeNode(Node *node, int newData)
{
    if (node == NULL)
        return node;
    int compareValue = newData - node->data;
    if (compareValue > 0)
    {
        node->right = removeNode(node->right, newData);
    }
    else if (compareValue < 0)
    {
        node->left = removeNode(node->left, newData);
    }
    else if (node->left != NULL && node->right != NULL)
    {
        node->data = searchMinValue(node->right)->data;//Find the minimum node of the right
subtree to replace the current node
        node->right = removeNode(node->right, node->data);
    }
    else
    {
        node = (node->left != NULL) ? node->left : node->right;
    }
    return node;

}
```

```c
void insert(Node *node, int newData)
{
    if (root == NULL)
    {
        root = (Node*)malloc(sizeof(Node));
        root->data = newData;
        root->left = NULL;
        root->right = NULL;
        return;
    }

    int compareValue = newData - node->data;

    //Recursive left subtree, continue to find the insertion position
    if (compareValue < 0)
    {
        if (node->left == NULL)
        {
            node->left = createNewNode(newData);
        }
        else
        {
            insert(node->left, newData);
        }
    }
    else if (compareValue > 0)
    {
        //Recursive right subtree, continue to find the insertion position
        if (node->right == NULL)
        {

            node->right = createNewNode(newData);
        }
        else
        {
            insert(node->right, newData);
        }
    }
}
```

```c
void freeMemery(Node *node)
{
    if (node == NULL)
    {
        return;
    }
    freeMemery(node->left); // Traversing the left subtree
    freeMemery(node->right); // Traversing the right subtree
    free(node);
}

int main()
{//Constructing a binary search tree
    insert(root, 60);
    insert(root, 40);
    insert(root, 20);
    insert(root, 10);
    insert(root, 30);
    insert(root, 50);
    insert(root, 80);
    insert(root, 70);
    insert(root, 90);
    printf("\ndelete node is:  10 \n");
    removeNode(root, 10);

    printf("\nIn-order traversal binary tree \n");
    inOrder(root);

    printf("\n----------------------------------------\n");
    printf("\ndelete node is:  20 \n");
    removeNode(root, 20);

    printf("\nIn-order traversal binary tree \n");
    inOrder(root);

    printf("\n----------------------------------------\n");
    printf("\ndelete node is:  40 \n");
    removeNode(root, 40);

    printf("\nIn-order traversal binary tree \n");
    inOrder(root);
    freeMemery(root);
    return 0;
}
```

Result:

delete node is: 10

In-order traversal binary tree
20, 30, 40, 50, 60, 70, 80, 90,
----

delete node is: 20

In-order traversal binary tree
30, 40, 50, 60, 70, 80, 90,
----

delete node is: 40

In-order traversal binary tree
30, 50, 60, 70, 80, 90,

Binary Heap Sorting

Binary Heap Sorting:
The value of the non-terminal node in the binary tree is not greater than the value of its left and right child nodes.

Small top heap : ki <= k2i and ki <= k2i+1
Big top heap :ki >= k2i and ki >= k2i+1

Parent node subscript = (i-1)/2
Left subnode subscript = 2*i+1
Right subnode subscript = 2*i+2

Heap sorting process:
1. Build a heap
2. After outputting the top element of the heap, adjust from top to bottom, compare the top element with the root node of its left and right subtrees, and swap the smallest element to the top of the heap; then adjust continuously until the leaf nodes to get new heap.

1. {10, 90, 20, 80, 30, 70, 40, 60, 50} **build heap and then heap sort output.**

Initialize the heap and build the heap

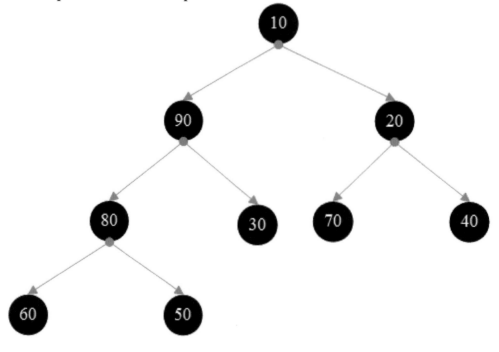

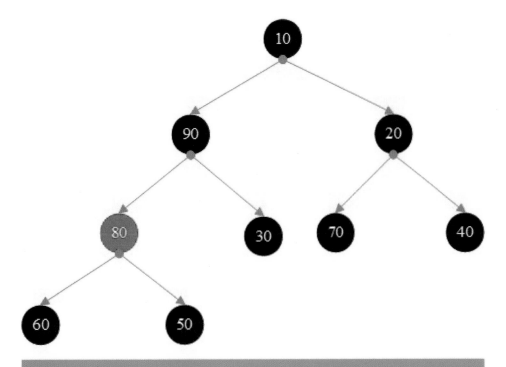

Not Leaf Node = 80 > left = 60 ,   80 > right = 50 No need to move

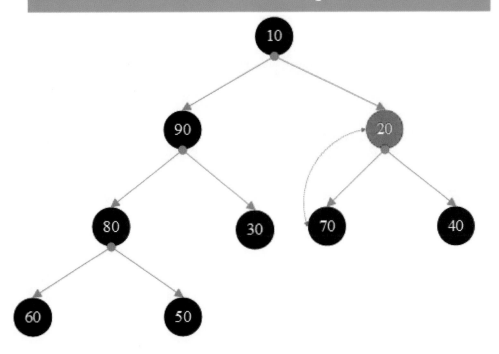

Not Leaf Node = 20 < left = 70 , 70 > right = 40 , 20 swap with 70

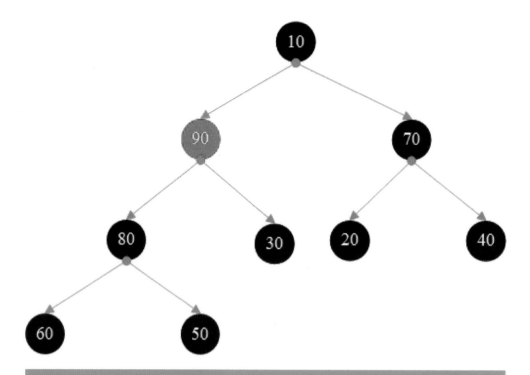

Not Leaf Node = 90 > left = 80 ,   80 > right = 30 No need to move

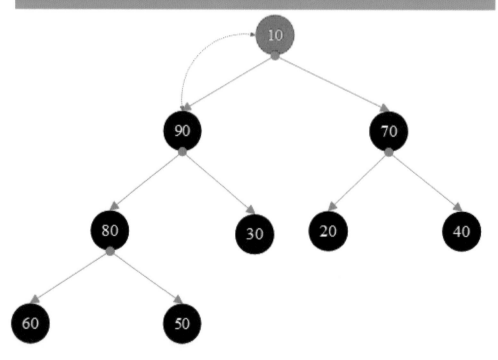

Not Leaf Node = 10 < left = 90 , 90 > right = 70   , 10 swap with 90

170

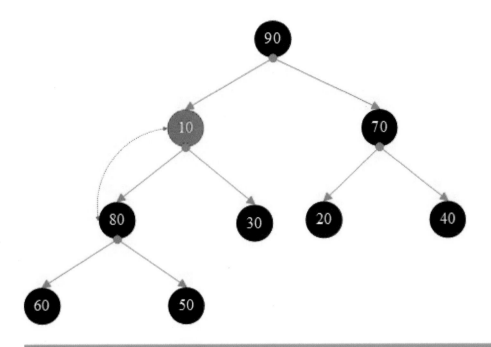

Still Not Leaf Node = 10 < left = 80 , 80 > right =30 , 10 swap with 80

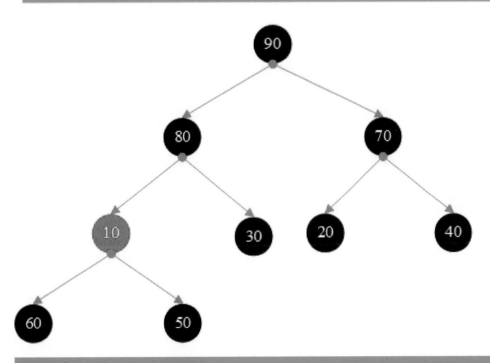

Still Not Leaf Node = 10 < left = 60 , 60 > right =50 , 10 swap with 60

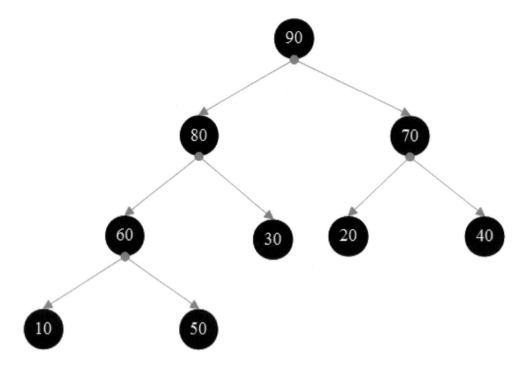

Create the heap finished

2. Start heap sorting

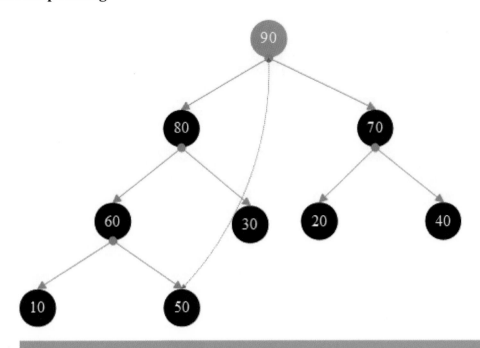

root = 90 and tail = 50 are exchanged

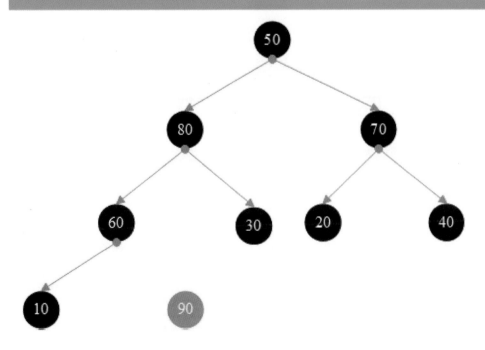

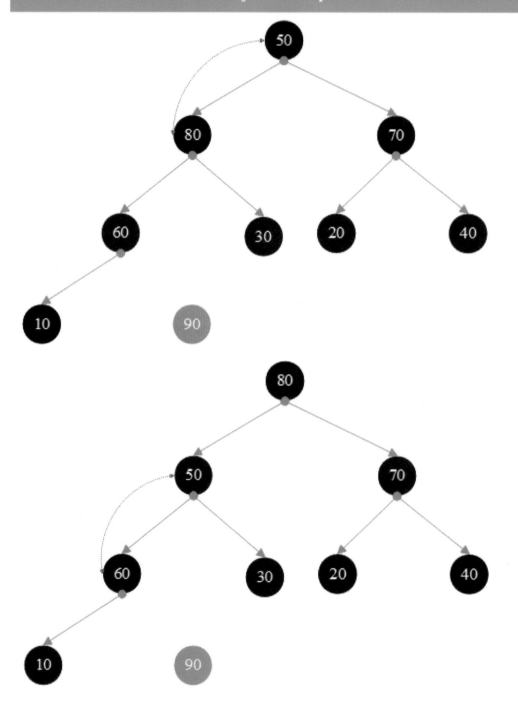

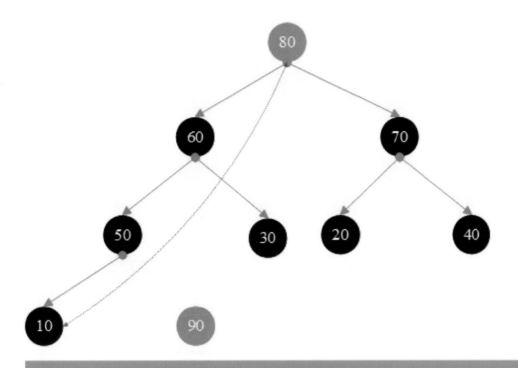

root = 80 and tail = 10 are exchanged

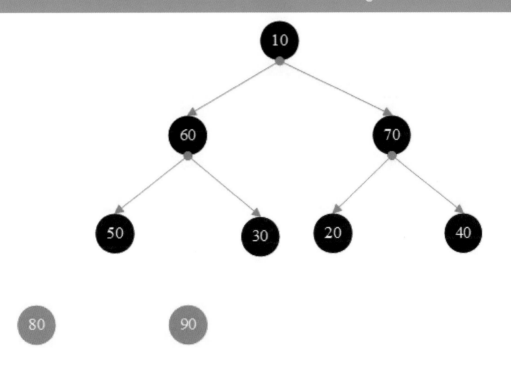

175

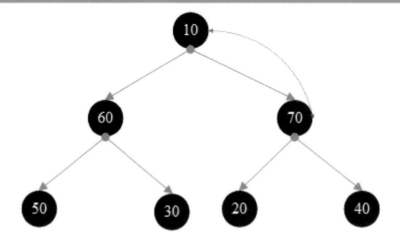

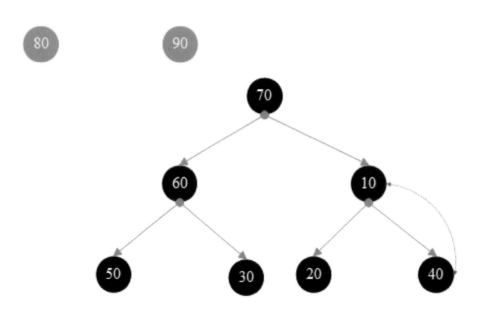

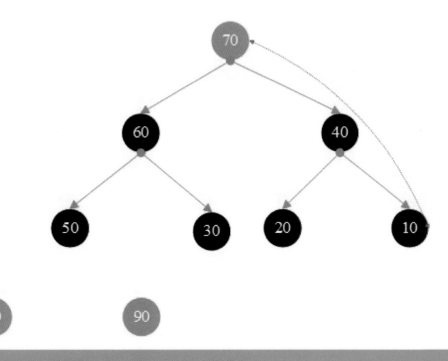

root = 70 and tail = 10 are exchanged

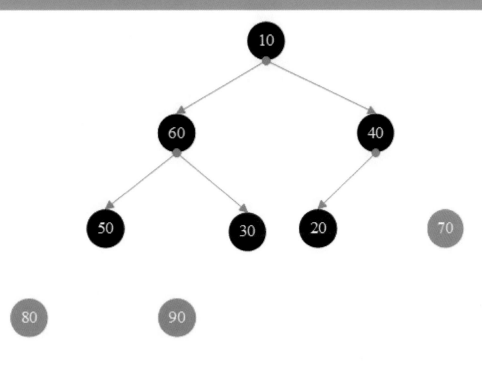

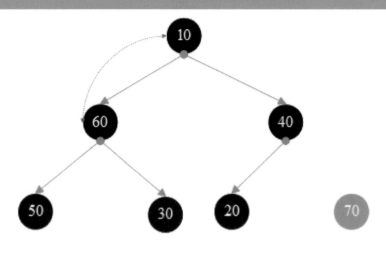

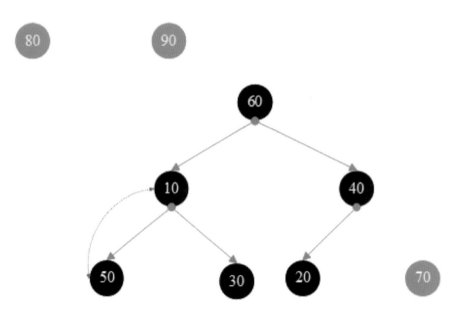

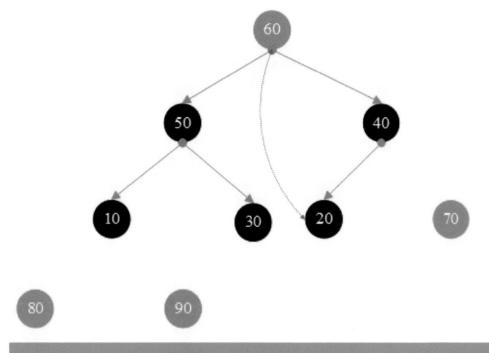

root = 60 and tail = 20 are exchanged

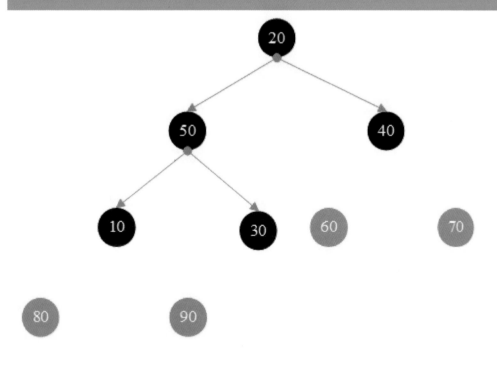

179

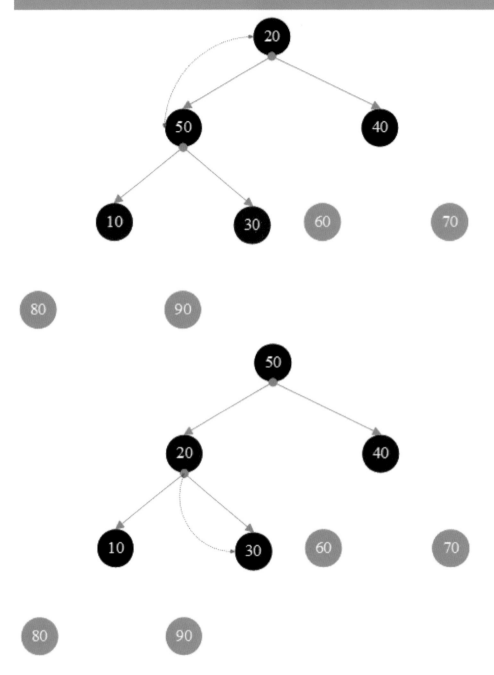

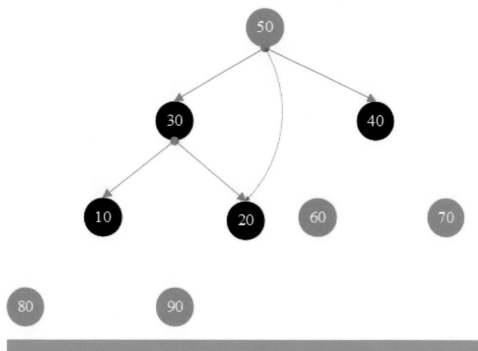

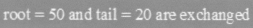

root = 50 and tail = 20 are exchanged

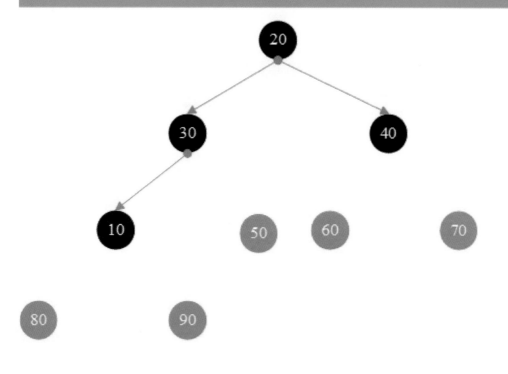

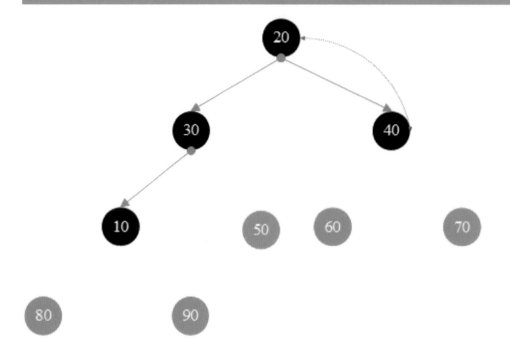

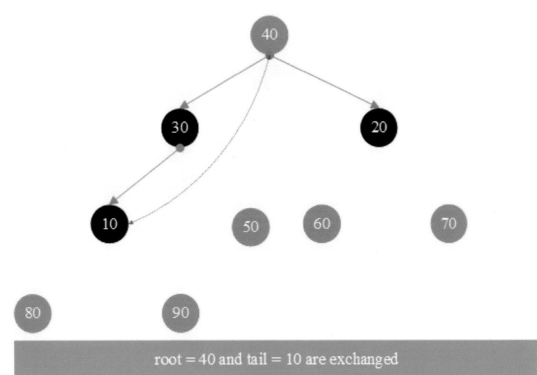

root = 40 and tail = 10 are exchanged

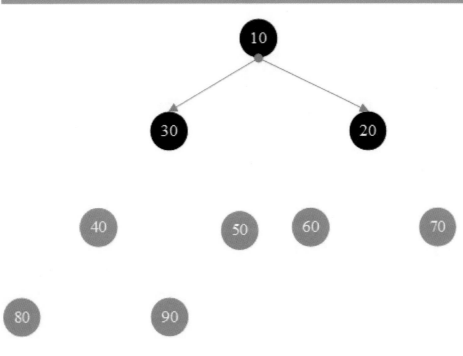

183

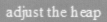

adjust the heap

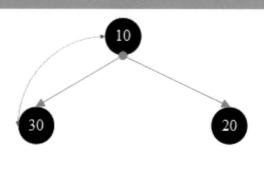

40 50 60 70

80 90

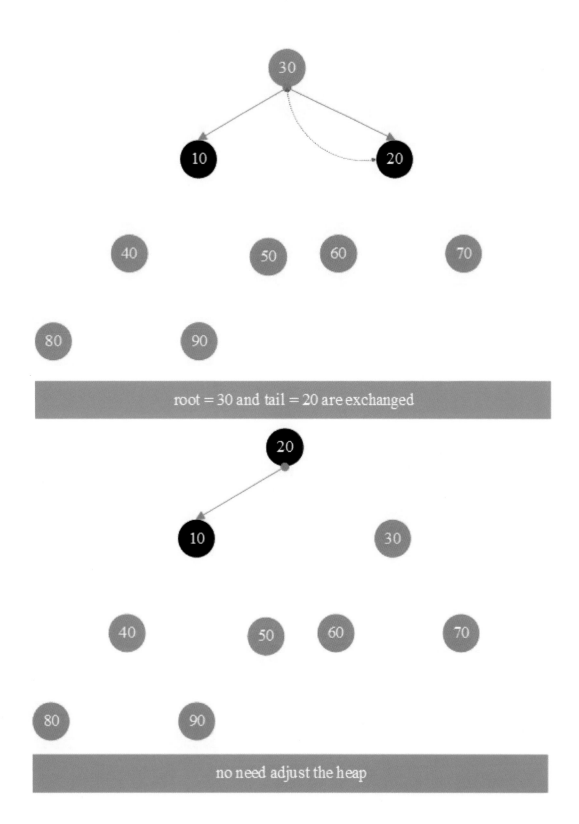

root = 30 and tail = 20 are exchanged

no need adjust the heap

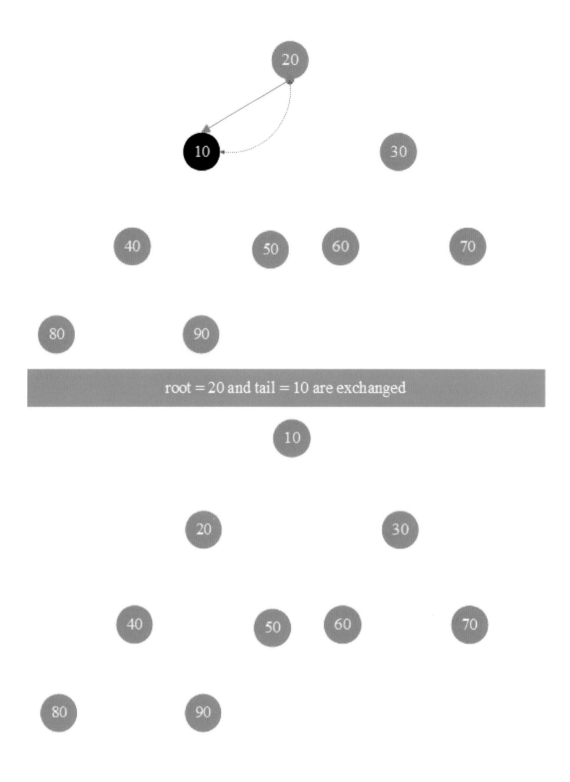

root = 20 and tail = 10 are exchanged

Heap sort result

HeapSort.c

```c
#include <stdio.h>

//Adjustment heap
void adjustHeap(int array[], int currentIndex, int maxLength)
{
    int noLeafValue = array[currentIndex]; // Current non-leaf node

    //2 * currentIndex + 1  Current left subtree subscript
    int j;
    for (j = 2 * currentIndex + 1; j <= maxLength; j = currentIndex * 2 + 1)
    {
        if (j < maxLength && array[j] < array[j + 1])
        {
            j++; // j Large subscript
        }

        if (noLeafValue >= array[j])
        {
            break;
        }

        array[currentIndex] = array[j]; // Move up to the parent node
        currentIndex = j;
    }

    array[currentIndex] = noLeafValue; // To put in the position
}
```

```c
//Initialize the heap
void createHeap(int array[], int length)
{
    // Build a heap, (length - 1) / 2 scan half of the nodes with child nodes
    int i;
    for (i = (length - 1) / 2; i >= 0; i--)
    {
        adjustHeap(array, i, length - 1);
    }
}

void heapSort(int array[], int length)
{
    int i;
    for (i = length - 1; i > 0; i--)
    {
        int temp = array[0];
        array[0] = array[i];
        array[i] = temp;
        adjustHeap(array, 0, i - 1);
    }
}

int main()
{
    int scores[] = { 10, 90, 20, 80, 30, 70, 40, 60, 50 };
    int length = sizeof(scores) / sizeof(scores[0]);

    printf("Before building a heap : \n");
    int i;
    for (i = 0; i < length; i++)
    {
        printf("%d, ", scores[i]);
    }
    printf("\n\n");
```

```
//////////////////////////////////////////////////////////

    printf("After building a heap : \n");
    createHeap(scores, length);
    for (i = 0; i < length; i++)
    {
        printf("%d, ", scores[i]);
    }
    printf("\n\n");

//////////////////////////////////////////////////////////

    printf("After heap sorting : \n");
    heapSort(scores, length);
    for (i = 0; i < length; i++)
    {
        printf("%d, ", scores[i]);
    }

    return 0;
}
```

Result:

Before building a heap :
10, 90, 20, 80, 30, 70, 40, 60, 50,

After building a heap :
90, 80, 70, 60, 30, 20, 40, 10, 50,

After heap sorting :
10, 20, 30, 40, 50, 60, 70, 80, 90,

Hash Table

Hash Table:

Access by mapping key => values in the table.

1. Map {19, 18, 35,40,41,42} to the HashTable mapping rule key % 4

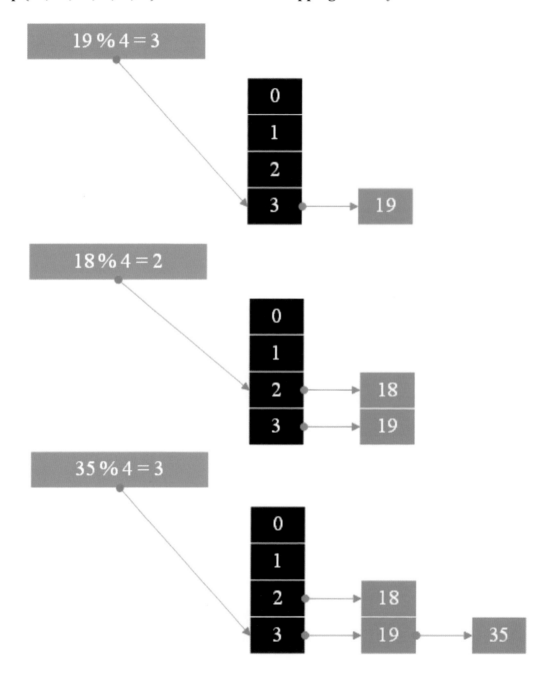

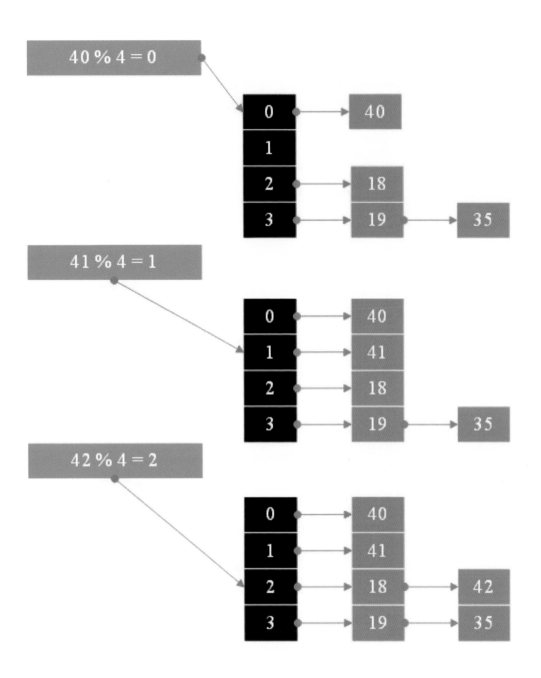

2. Implement a Hashtable

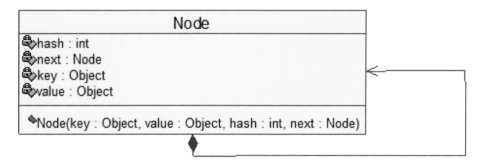

```
typedef struct Node
{
    char *key;
    char *value;
    int hash;
    struct Node *next;
} Node;
```

Hashtable.c

```c
#include <stdio.h>
#include<stdlib.h>
#include<math.h>
#include<string.h>

#define TRUE 1
#define FALSE 0
#define CAPACITY 16

typedef struct Node
{
    char *key;
    char *value;
    int hash;
    struct Node *next;

} Node;

Node *table[CAPACITY];
int size;

int isEmpty()
{
    return size == 0 ? TRUE : FALSE;
}

int hashCode(char *key)
{
    int num = 0;
    int i;
    char ch;
    for( i=0; ch = *(key+i); i++)
    {
        num += (int)ch;
    }
    //hash strategy is to take the square in the middle
    double avg = num * (pow(5, 0.5) - 1) / 2;
    double numeric = avg - floor(avg);
    return (int)floor(numeric * CAPACITY);
}
```

```c
void put(char *key, char *value)
{
    int hash = hashCode(key);
    Node *newNode = NULL;
    newNode = (Node*)malloc(sizeof(Node));
    newNode->key = key;
    newNode->value = value;
    newNode->hash = hash;
    newNode->next = NULL;

    Node *node = table[hash];
    while (node != NULL)
    {
        if (strcmp(node->key, key) == 0)
        {
            node->value = value;
            return;
        }
        node = node->next;
    }
    newNode->next = table[hash];
    table[hash] = newNode;
    size++;
}

char* get(char *key)
{
    if (key == NULL)
    {
        return NULL;
    }
    int hash = hashCode(key);
    Node *node = table[hash];
    while (node != NULL)
    {
        if (strcmp(node->key, key) == 0)
        {
            return node->value;
        }
        node = node->next;
    }
    return NULL;
}
```

```c
void freeMemery()
{
    int i;
    for(i=0; i<CAPACITY; i++)
    {
        Node *node = table[i];
        while (node!= NULL)
        {
            Node *temp = node->next;
            node = node->next;
            free(temp);
        }
        free(node);
    }
}

int main()
{
    put("david", "Good Boy Keep Going");
    put("grace", "Cute Girl Keep Going");

    printf("david => %s \n", get("david"));
    printf("grace => %s \n", get("grace"));

    freeMemery();

    return 0;
}
```

Result:

david => Good Boy Keep Going
grace => Cute Girl Keep Going

Directed Graph and Depth-First Search

Directed Graph:

The data structure is represented by an adjacency matrix (that is, a two-dimensional array) and an adjacency list. Each node is called a vertex, and two adjacent nodes are called edges.

Directed Graph has direction : A -> B and B -> A are different

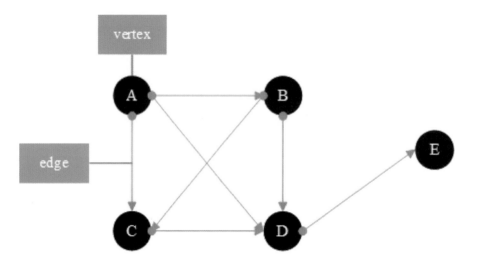

1. The adjacency matrix is described above:

The total number of vertices is a two-dimensional array size, if have value of the edge is 1, otherwise no value of the edge is 0.

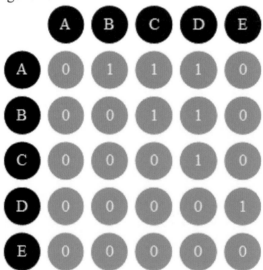

2. Depth-First Search:

Look for the neighboring edge node B from A and then find the neighboring node C from B and so on until all nodes are found A -> B -> C -> D -> E.

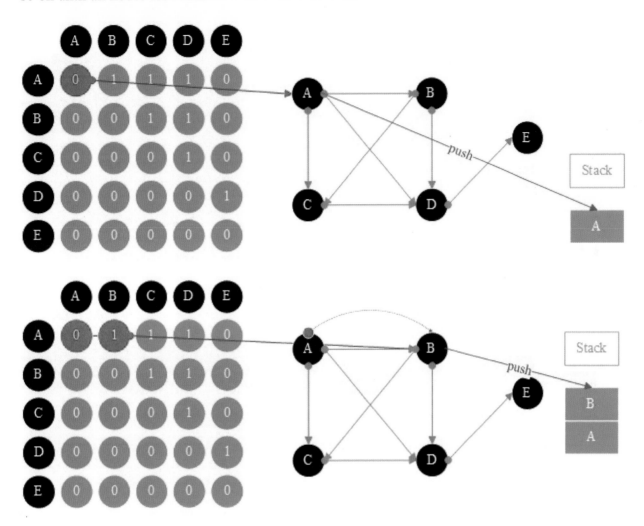

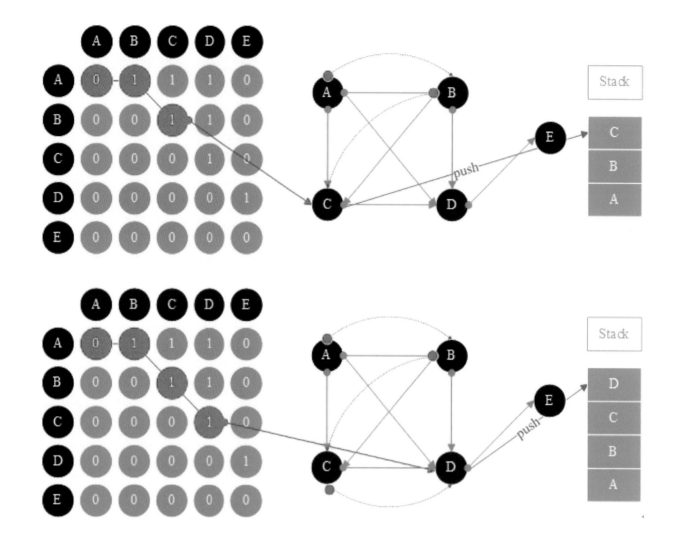

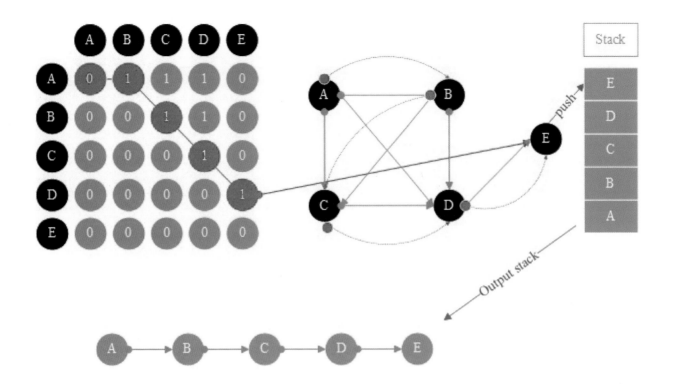

Graph.c

```c
#include <stdio.h>
#include<stdlib.h>
#include<math.h>
#include<string.h>

#define TRUE 1
#define FALSE 0
#define MAX_VERTEX_SIZE  5
#define STACKSIZE  1000

typedef struct Vertex
{
    char *data;
    int visited; // Have you visited
} Vertex;

// Stack saves current vertices
int top = -1;
int stacks[STACKSIZE];

push(int element)
{
    top++;
    stacks[top] = element;
}

int pop()
{
    if(top == -1)
    {
        return -1;
    }

    int data = stacks[top];
    top--;
    return data;
}
```

```c
int peek()
{
    if(top == -1)
    {
        return -1;
    }

    int data = stacks[top];
    return data;
}

int isEmpty()
{
    if(top <= -1)
    {
        return TRUE;
    }
    return FALSE;
}
////// stack end //////////////////////////


int size = 0; // Current vertex size
Vertex vertexs[MAX_VERTEX_SIZE];
int adjacencyMatrix[MAX_VERTEX_SIZE][MAX_VERTEX_SIZE];

void addVertex(char *data)
{
    Vertex vertex;
    vertex.data = data;
    vertex.visited = FALSE;

    vertexs[size] = vertex;
    size++;
}

// Add adjacent edges
void addEdge(int from, int to)
{
    // A -> B != B -> A
    adjacencyMatrix[from][to] = 1;
}
```

```c
// Clear reset
void clear()
{
    int i;
    for (i = 0; i < size; i++)
    {
        vertexs[i].visited = FALSE;
    }
}

void depthFirstSearch()
{
    // Start searching from the first vertex
    vertexs[0].visited = TRUE;
    printf("%s", vertexs[0].data);
    push(0);

    while (!isEmpty())
    {
        int row = peek();
        // Get adjacent vertex positions that have not been visited
        int col = findAdjacencyUnVisitedVertex(row);
        if (col == -1)
        {
            pop();
        }
        else
        {
            vertexs[col].visited = TRUE;
            printf(" -> %s", vertexs[col].data);
            push(col);
        }
    }

    clear();
}
```

```c
// Get adjacent vertex positions that have not been visited
int findAdjacencyUnVisitedVertex(int row)
{
    int col;
    for (col = 0; col < size; col++)
    {
        if (adjacencyMatrix[row][col] == 1 && !vertexs[col].visited)
        {
            return col;
        }
    }

    return -1;
}

void printGraph()
{
    printf("Two-dimensional array traversal vertex edge and adjacent array : \n ");
    int i;
    for (i = 0; i < MAX_VERTEX_SIZE; i++)
    {
        printf("%s ",vertexs[i].data);
    }
    printf("\n");

    for (i = 0; i < MAX_VERTEX_SIZE; i++)
    {
        printf("%s ", vertexs[i].data);
        int j;
        for (j = 0; j < MAX_VERTEX_SIZE; j++)
        {
            printf("%d ", adjacencyMatrix[i][j]);
        }
        printf("\n");
    }
}
```

```
int main()
{
    addVertex("A");
    addVertex("B");
    addVertex("C");
    addVertex("D");
    addVertex("E");

    addEdge(0, 1);
    addEdge(0, 2);
    addEdge(0, 3);
    addEdge(1, 2);
    addEdge(1, 3);
    addEdge(2, 3);
    addEdge(3, 4);

    // Two-dimensional array traversal output vertex edge and adjacent array
    printGraph();

    printf("\nDepth-first search traversal output : \n");
    depthFirstSearch();
    return 0;
}
```

Result:

```
  A B C D E
A 0 1 1 1 0
B 0 0 1 1 0
C 0 0 0 1 0
D 0 0 0 0 1
E 0 0 0 0 0
```

Depth-first search traversal output :
A -> B -> C -> D -> E

Directed Graph and Breadth-First Search

Breadth-First Search:
Find all neighboring edge nodes B, C, D from A and then find all neighboring nodes A, C, D
from B and so on until all nodes are found A -> B -> C -> D -> E.

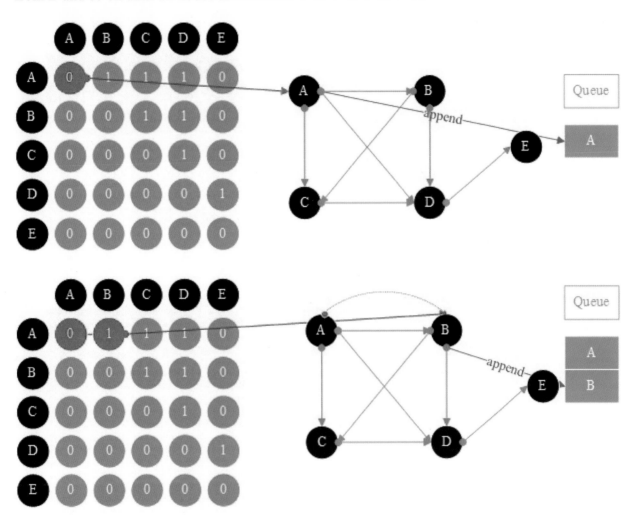

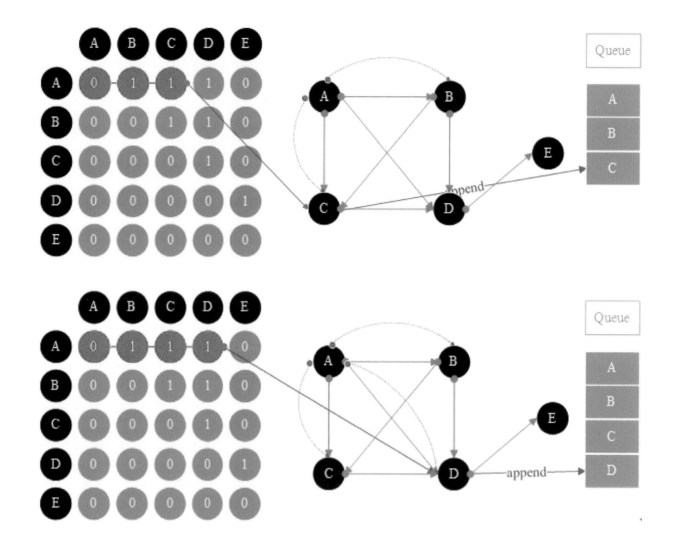

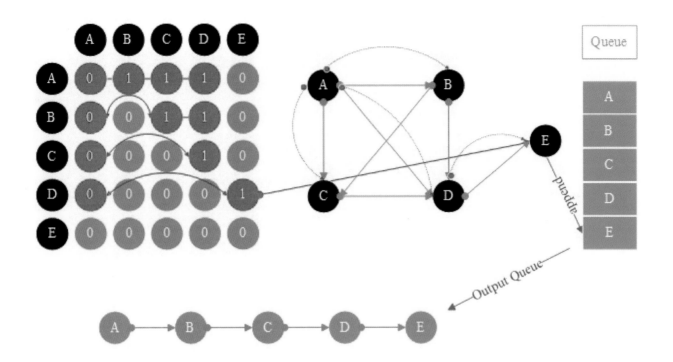

Graph.c

```c
#include <stdio.h>
#include<stdlib.h>

#define TRUE 1
#define FALSE 0
#define MAX_VERTEX_SIZE  5

// Queue saves current vertices

#define QUEUESIZE 40

typedef struct{
   int queue[QUEUESIZE];
   int head,tail;
} Queue ;

Queue *q;

void initQueue()
{
   q = (Queue*)malloc(sizeof(Queue));
   q->head = q->tail = 0;
}

int isQueueEmpty()
{
   if(q->head == q->tail)
   {
      return TRUE;
   }
   else
   {
      return FALSE;
   }
}
```

```c
int enQueue(int data){
    if(q->tail == QUEUESIZE){
        printf("The queue was full and could not join.\n");
        return 0;
    }

    q->queue[q->tail++] = data;
    return TRUE;
}

int deleteQueue(){
    if(q->head == q->tail){
        printf("The queue was empty and could not join.\n");
        return 0;
    }
    int data = q->queue[q->head++];
    return data;
}

////// queue end //////////////////////////

typedef struct Vertex
{
    char *data;
    int visited; // Have you visited
} Vertex;

int size = 0; // Current vertex size
Vertex vertexs[MAX_VERTEX_SIZE];
int adjacencyMatrix[MAX_VERTEX_SIZE][MAX_VERTEX_SIZE];

void addVertex(char *data)
{
    Vertex vertex;
    vertex.data = data;
    vertex.visited = FALSE;

    vertexs[size] = vertex;
    size++;
}
```

```c
// Add adjacent edges
void addEdge(int from, int to)
{
    // A -> B != B -> A
    adjacencyMatrix[from][to] = 1;
}

// Clear reset
void clear()
{
    int i;
    for (i = 0; i < size; i++)
    {
        vertexs[i].visited = FALSE;
    }
}

void breadthFirstSearch()
{
    // Start searching from the first vertex
    vertexs[0].visited = TRUE;
    printf("%s", vertexs[0].data);
    enQueue(0);

    int col;
    while (!isQueueEmpty())
    {
        int row = deleteQueue();
    // Get adjacent vertex positions that have not been visited
        col = findAdjacencyUnVisitedVertex(row);
        //Loop through all vertices connected to the current vertex
        while (col != -1)
        {
            vertexs[col].visited = TRUE;
            printf(" -> %s", vertexs[col].data);
            enQueue(col);
            col = findAdjacencyUnVisitedVertex(row);
        }
    }
    clear();
}
```

```c
// Get adjacent vertex positions that have not been visited
int findAdjacencyUnVisitedVertex(int row)
{
    int col;
    for (col = 0; col < size; col++)
    {
        if (adjacencyMatrix[row][col] == 1 && !vertexs[col].visited)
        {
            return col;
        }
    }
    return -1;
}

void printGraph()
{
    printf("Two-dimensional array traversal vertex edge and adjacent array : \n ");
    int i;
    for (i = 0; i < MAX_VERTEX_SIZE; i++)
    {
        printf("%s ",vertexs[i].data);
    }
    printf("\n");

    for (i = 0; i < MAX_VERTEX_SIZE; i++)
    {
        printf("%s ", vertexs[i].data);
        int j;
        for (j = 0; j < MAX_VERTEX_SIZE; j++)
        {
            printf("%d ", adjacencyMatrix[i][j]);
        }
        printf("\n");
    }
}
```

```c
int main()
{
    initQueue();

    addVertex("A");
    addVertex("B");
    addVertex("C");
    addVertex("D");
    addVertex("E");

    addEdge(0, 1);
    addEdge(0, 2);
    addEdge(0, 3);
    addEdge(1, 2);
    addEdge(1, 3);
    addEdge(2, 3);
    addEdge(3, 4);

    // Two-dimensional array traversal output vertex edge and adjacent array
    printGraph();

    printf("\nBreadth-first search traversal output : \n");
    breadthFirstSearch();

    free(q);
    return 0;
}
```

Result:

```
  A B C D E
A 0 1 1 1 0
B 0 0 1 1 0
C 0 0 0 1 0
D 0 0 0 0 1
E 0 0 0 0 0
```

Breadth-first search traversal output :
A -> B -> C -> D -> E

Directed Graph Topological Sorting

Directed Graph Topological Sorting:
Sort the vertices in the directed graph with order of direction

.
Directed Graph has direction : A -> B and B -> A are different

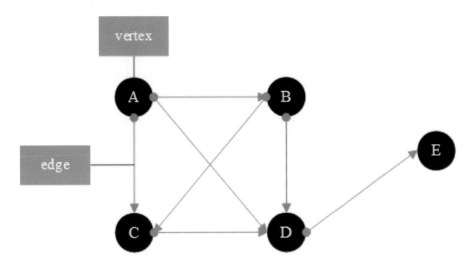

1. The adjacency matrix is described above:

The total number of vertices is a two-dimensional array size, if have value of the edge is 1, otherwise no value of the edge is 0.

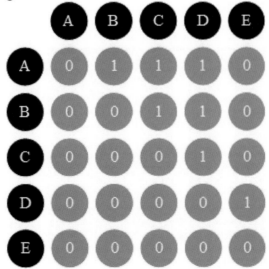

Topological sorting from vertex A : A -> B -> C -> D -> E

Find no successor vertices E then save to topologys, last E remove from the graph

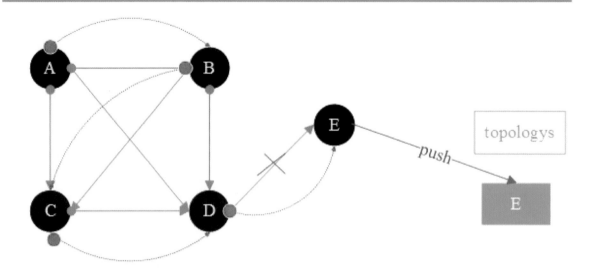

Find no successor vertices D then save to topologys, last D remove from the graph

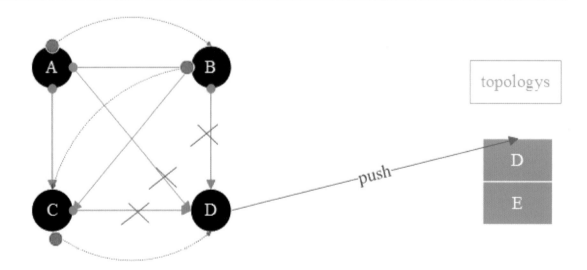

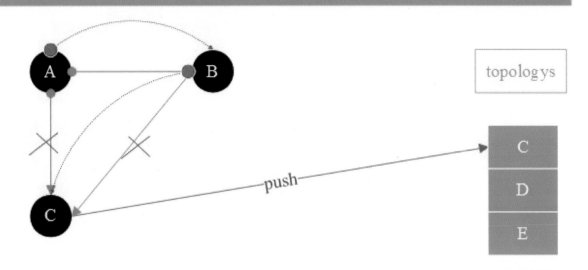

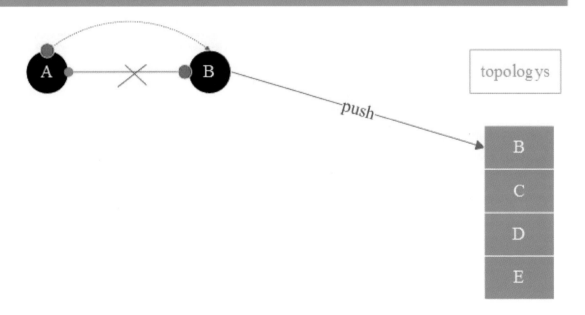

Find no successor vertices C then save to topologys, last C remove from the graph

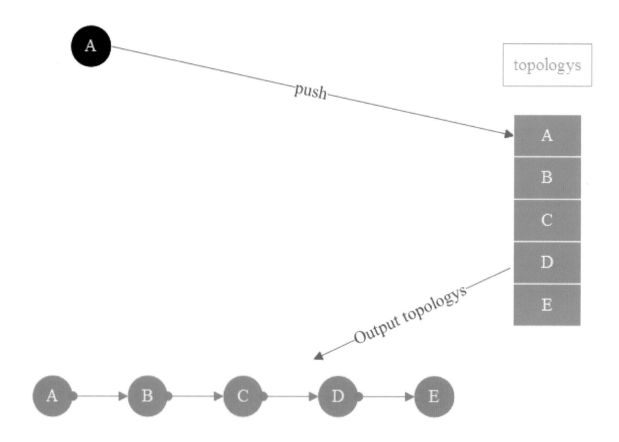

Topology.c

```c
#include <stdio.h>
#include<stdlib.h>
#include<math.h>
#include<string.h>

#define TRUE 1
#define FALSE 0
#define MAX_VERTEX_SIZE  5
#define STACKSIZE  1000

typedef struct Vertex
{
   char *data;
   int visited; // Have you visited
} Vertex;

// Stack saves current vertices
int top = -1;
int stacks[STACKSIZE];

push(int element)
{
   top++;
   stacks[top] = element;
}

int pop()
{
   if(top == -1)
   {
      return -1;
   }
   int data = stacks[top];
   top--;
   return data;
}
```

```c
int peek()
{
    if(top == -1)
    {
        return -1;
    }
    int data = stacks[top];
    return data;
}

int isEmpty()
{
    if(top <= -1)
    {
        return TRUE;
    }
    return FALSE;
}
////// stack end ///////////////////////////

int size = 0; // Current vertex size
Vertex vertexs[MAX_VERTEX_SIZE];
// An array of topological sort results, recording the sorted sequence number of each node.
Vertex topologys[MAX_VERTEX_SIZE];

int adjacencyMatrix[MAX_VERTEX_SIZE][MAX_VERTEX_SIZE];

void addVertex(char *data)
{
    Vertex vertex;
    vertex.data = data;
    vertex.visited = FALSE;

    vertexs[size] = vertex;
    size++;
}
```

```
// Add adjacent edges
void addEdge(int from, int to)
{
    // A -> B = B -> A
    adjacencyMatrix[from][to] = 1;
}

void removeVertex(int vertex)
{
    if (vertex != size - 1)
    {
        //If the vertex is the last element, the end
        int i;
        for (i = vertex; i < size - 1; i++)
        {// The vertices are removed from the vertex array
            vertexs[i] = vertexs[i + 1];
        }

        int row;
        int col;
        for (row = vertex; row < size - 1; row++)
        {
            // move up a row
            for (col = 0; col < size - 1; col++)
            {
                adjacencyMatrix[row][col] = adjacencyMatrix[row + 1][col];
            }
        }

        for (col = vertex; col < size - 1; col++)
        {// move left a row
            for (row = 0; row < size - 1; row++)
            {
                adjacencyMatrix[row][col] = adjacencyMatrix[row][col + 1];
            }
        }
    }
    size--;// Decrease the number of vertices
}
```

```c
void topologySort()
{
    while (size > 0)
    {
        int noSuccessorVertex = getNoSuccessorVertex();// Get a no successor node
        if (noSuccessorVertex == -1)
        {
            printf("There is ring in Graph \n");
            return;
        }
        topologys[size - 1] = vertexs[noSuccessorVertex];// Copy the deleted node to the sorted array
        removeVertex(noSuccessorVertex);// Delete no successor node
    }
}

int getNoSuccessorVertex()
{
    int existSuccessor = FALSE;
    int row;
    for (row = 0; row < size; row++)
    {// For each vertex
        existSuccessor = FALSE;
        //If the node has a fixed row, each column has a 1, indicating that the node has a
        successor, terminating the loop
        int col;
        for (col = 0; col < size; col++)
        {
            if (adjacencyMatrix[row][col] == 1)
            {
                existSuccessor = TRUE;
                break;
            }
        }

        if (!existSuccessor)
        {// If the node has no successor, return its subscript
            return row;
        }
    }
    return -1;
}
```

```c
void printGraph()
{
    printf("Two-dimensional array traversal vertex edge and adjacent array :  \n  ");
    int i;
    for (i = 0; i < MAX_VERTEX_SIZE; i++)
    {
        printf("%s  ",vertexs[i].data);
    }
    printf("\n");

    for (i = 0; i < MAX_VERTEX_SIZE; i++)
    {
        printf("%s  ", vertexs[i].data);
        int j;
        for (j = 0; j < MAX_VERTEX_SIZE; j++)
        {
            printf("%d  ", adjacencyMatrix[i][j]);
        }
        printf("\n");
    }
}

int main()
{
    addVertex("A");
    addVertex("B");
    addVertex("C");
    addVertex("D");
    addVertex("E");

    addEdge(0, 1);
    addEdge(0, 2);
    addEdge(0, 3);
    addEdge(1, 2);
    addEdge(1, 3);
    addEdge(2, 3);
    addEdge(3, 4);
```

```
// Two-dimensional array traversal output vertex edge and adjacent array
printGraph();

printf("\nDepth-First Search traversal output : \n");
printf("Directed Graph Topological Sorting: \n");
topologySort();
int i;
for (i = 0; i < MAX_VERTEX_SIZE; i++)
{
    printf("%s -> ", topologys[i].data);
}

return 0;
}
```

Result:

Two-dimensional array traversal output vertex edge and adjacent array :
```
  A B C D E
A 0 1 1 1 0
B 0 0 1 1 0
C 0 0 0 1 0
D 0 0 0 0 1
E 0 0 0 0 0
```

Depth-First Search traversal output :
Directed Graph Topological Sorting:
A -> B -> C -> D -> E ->

Towers of Hanoi

The Hanoi Tower that a Frenchman M. Claus (Lucas) from Thailand to France in 1883. Hanoi Tower which is supported by three diamond Pillars. At the beginning, God placed 64 gold discs from top to bottom on the first Pillar. God ordered the monks to move all gold discs from the first Pillar to the third Pillar. The principle of large plates under small plates during the handling process. If only one plate is moved daily, the tower will be destroyed. when all the discs are moved that is the end of the world.

Let's turn this story into an algorithm:

Mark the three columns as ABC.
1. If there is only one disc, move it directly to C (A->C).
2. When there are two discs, use B as an auxiliary (A->B, A->C,B->C).
3. If there are more than two discs, use B as an auxiliary(A->B, A->C,B->C), and continue to recursive process.

1. If there is only one disc, move it directly to C (A->C).

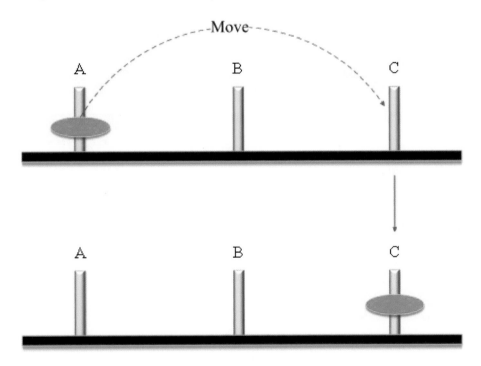

2. When there are two discs, use B as an auxiliary (A->B, A->C,B->C).

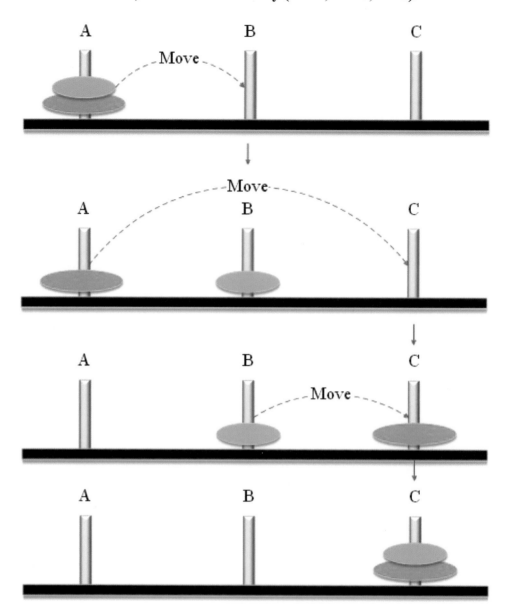

3. If more than two discs, use B as an auxiliary, and continue to recursive process.

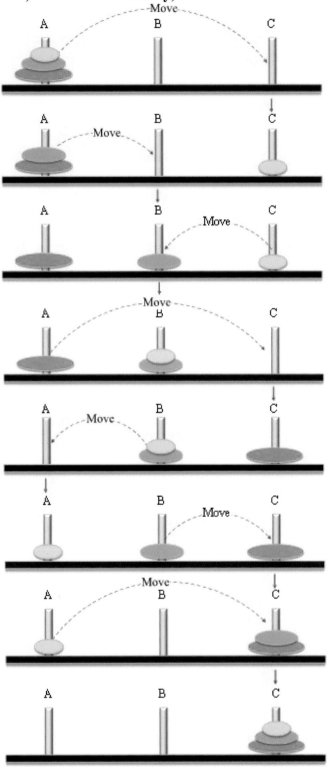

TowersOfHanoi.c

```c
#include <stdio.h>
void hanoi(int n, char A, char B, char C)
{
    if (n == 1)
    {
        printf("Move %d %c to %c \n", n, A, C);
    }
    else
    {
        hanoi(n - 1, A, C, B); // Move the n-1th disc on the A  through C to  B
        printf("Move %d from %c to %c \n", n, A, C);
        hanoi(n - 1, B, A, C); //Move the n-1th disc on the B  through  A to  C
    }
}

int main()
{
    printf("Please enter the number of discs : \n");
    int n;
    scanf("%d", &n);
    hanoi(n, 'A', 'B', 'C');
    return 0;
}
```

Result:
```
Please enter the number of discs :
1
Move 1 A  to C

Please enter the number of discs :
2
Move 1 A  to B
Move 2 from A  to C
Move 1 B  to C

Please enter the number of discs :
3
Move 1 A  to C
Move 2 from A  to B
Move 1 C  to B
Move 3 from A  to C
Move 1 B  to A
Move 2 from B  to C
Move 1 A  to C
```

Fibonacci

Fibonacci : a European mathematician in the 1200s, in his writings: "If there is a rabbit
After a month can birth to a newborn rabbit. At first there was only 1 rabbit, after one month still
1 rabbit. after two month 2 rabbit, and after three months there are 3 rabbit ......
for example: 1, 1, 2, 3, 5, 8, 13 ...

Fibonacci definition:

if n = 0, 1
   fn = n
if n > 1
   fn = fn-1 + fn-2

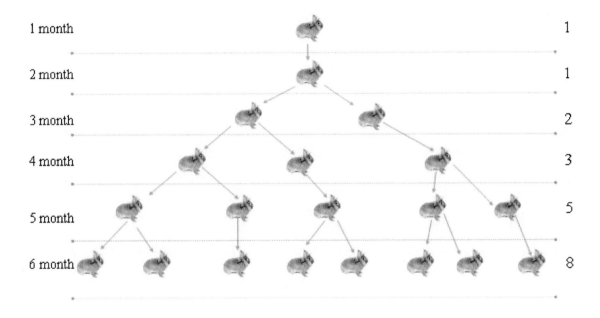

1 month	1
2 month	1
3 month	2
4 month	3
5 month	5
6 month	8

Fibonacci.c

```c
#include <stdio.h>
int fibonacci(int n)
{
    if (n == 1 || n == 2)
    {
        return 1;
    }
    else
    {
        return fibonacci(n - 1) + fibonacci(n - 2);
    }
}

int main()
{
    printf("Please enter the number of month : \n");
    int number;
    scanf("%d", &number);

    int i;
    for (i = 1; i <= number; i++)
    {
        printf("%d month: %d \n", i, fibonacci(i));
    }
    return 0;
}
```

Result:

```
Please enter the number of month :
7
1 month: 1
2 month: 1
3 month: 2
4 month: 3
5 month: 5
6 month: 8
7 month: 13
```

Dijkstra

The tricolor flag was originally raised by E.W. Dijkstra, who used the Dutch national flag (Dijkstra is Dutch).

Suppose there is a rope with red, white, and blue flags. At first all the flags on the rope are not in order. You need to arrange them in the order of blue -> white -> red. How to move them with the least times. you just only do this on the rope, and only swap two flags at a time.

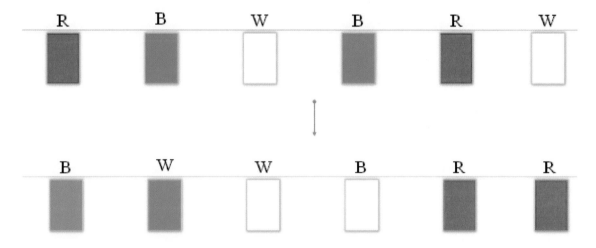

Solution:

Use the char arrays to store the flags. For example, b, w, and r indicate the position of **blue**, **white** and **red** flags. The beginning of b and w is 0 of the array, and r is at the end of the array.

(1) If the position of w is a blue flag, flags[w] exchange with flags[b]. And whiteIndex and b is moved backward by 1.
(2) If the position of w is a white flag, w moves backward by 1.
(3) If the position of w is a red flag, flags[w] exchange with flags[r]. r moves forward by 1.

In the end, the flags in front of b are all blue, and the flags behind r are all red.

Graphic Solution

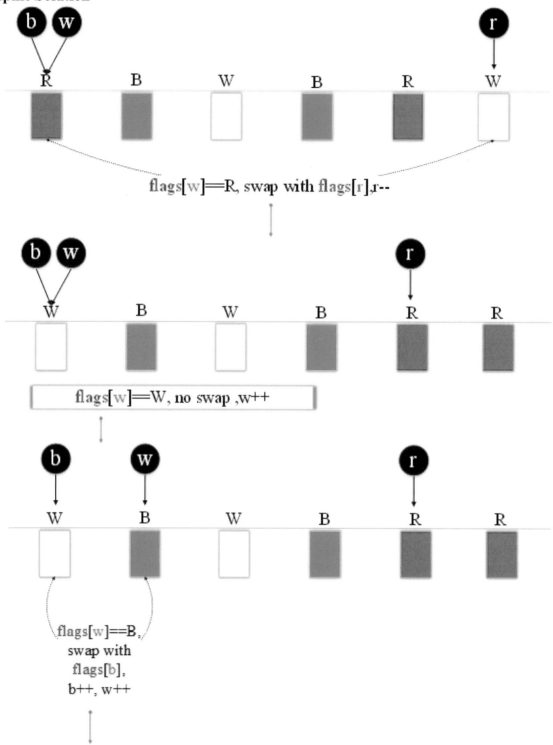

flags[w]==R, swap with flags[r],r--

flags[w]==W, no swap ,w++

flags[w]==B,
swap with
flags[b],
b++, w++

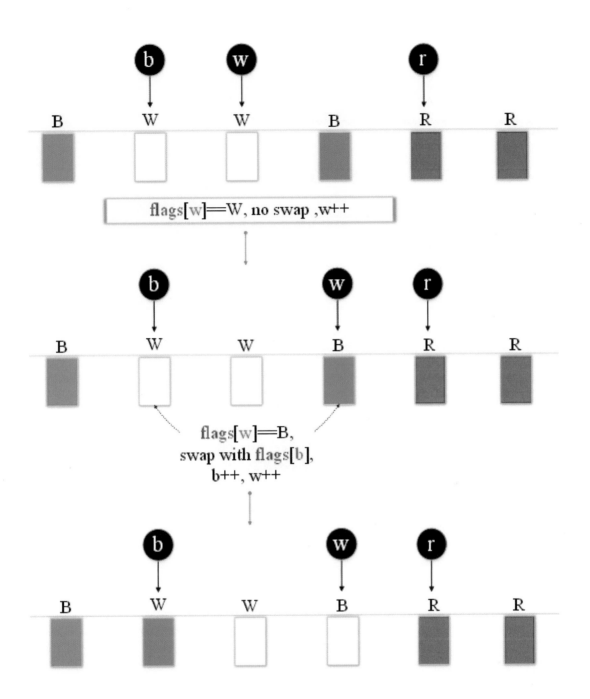

Dijkstra.c

```c
#include <stdio.h>
int main()
{
    char flags[] = { 'R', 'B', 'W', 'B', 'R', 'W' };
    int length = strlen(flags);
    int b = 0, w = 0, r = length - 1;
    int count = 0;
    while (w <= r)
    {
        if (flags[w] == 'W')
        {
            w++;
        }
        else if (flags[w] == 'B')
        {
            char temp = flags[w];
            flags[w] = flags[b];
            flags[b] = temp;
            w++;
            b++;
            count++;
        }
        else if (flags[w] == 'R')
        {
            char m = flags[w];
            flags[w] = flags[r];
            flags[r] = m;
            r--;
            count++;
        }
    }

    int i;
    for (i = 0; i < length; i++)
    {
        printf("%c",flags[i]);
    }
    printf("\nThe total exchange count : %d", count);
    return 0;
}
```

Result:
```
BBWWRR
The total exchange count : 4
```

Mouse Walking Maze

Mouse Walking Maze is a basic type of recursive solution. We use 2 to represent the wall in a two-dimensional array, and use 1 to represent the path of the mouse, and try to find the path from the entrance to the exit.

Solution:

The mouse moves in four directions: up, left, down, and right. if hit the wall go back and select the next forward direction, so test the four directions in the array until mouse reach the exit.

Graphic Solution

{ 2, 2, 2, 2, 2, 2, 2 }
{ 2, 0, 0, 0, 0, 0, 2 }
{ 2, 2, 2, 0, 2, 0, 2 }
{ 2, 0, 2, 0, 0, 2, 2 }
{ 2, 2, 0, 2, 0, 2, 2 }
{ 2, 0, 0, 0, 0, 0, 2 }
{ 2, 2, 2, 2, 2, 2, 2 }

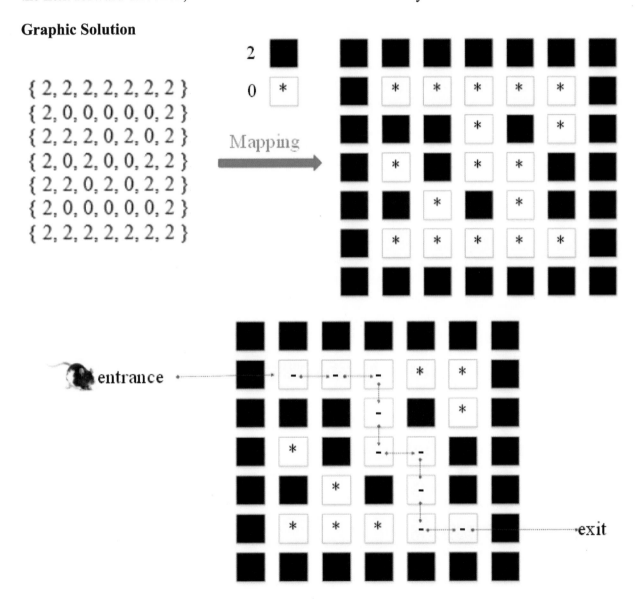

MouseWalkingMaze.c

```c
#include <stdio.h>

int maze[7][7] = {
   { 2, 2, 2, 2, 2, 2, 2 },
   { 2, 0, 0, 0, 0, 0, 2 },
   { 2, 2, 2, 0, 2, 0, 2 },
   { 2, 0, 2, 0, 0, 2, 2 },
   { 2, 2, 0, 2, 0, 2, 2 },
   { 2, 0, 0, 0, 0, 0, 2 },
   { 2, 2, 2, 2, 2, 2, 2 }
   };

int startI = 1;
int startJ = 1;
int endI = 5;
int endJ = 5;
int success = 0;

//The mouse moves in four directions: up, left, down, and right. if hit the wall go back and
select the next forward direction
int visit(int i, int j)
{
   maze[i][j] = 1;
   if (i == endI && j == endJ)
   {
      success = 1;
   }
   if (success != 1 && maze[i][j + 1] == 0)
      visit(i, j + 1);
   if (success != 1 && maze[i + 1][j] == 0)
      visit(i + 1, j);
   if (success != 1 && maze[i][j - 1] == 0)
      visit(i, j - 1);
   if (success != 1 && maze[i - 1][j] == 0)
      visit(i - 1, j);
   if (success != 1)
      maze[i][j] = 0;
   return success;
}
```

```c
int main()
{
    printf("Maze : \n");
    int i;
    int j;
    for (i = 0; i < 7; i++)
    {
        for (j = 0; j < 7; j++)
        {
            if (maze[i][j] == 2)
                printf("  ");
            else
                printf("* ");
        }
        printf("\n");
    }

    if (visit(startI, startJ) == 0)
    {
        printf("No exit found \n");
    }
    else
    {
        printf("Maze Path : \n");
        for (i = 0; i < 7; i++)
        {
            for (j = 0; j < 7; j++)
            {
                if (maze[i][j] == 2)
                    printf("  ");
                else if (maze[i][j] == 1)
                    printf("- ");
                else
                    printf("* ");
            }
            printf("\n");
        }
    }

    return 0;
}
```

Result:

```
Maze:
```

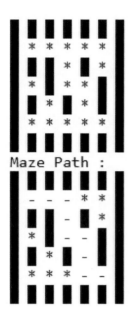

```
Maze Path :
```

Eight Coins

There are eight coins with the same appearance, one is a counterfeit coin, and the weight of counterfeit coin is different from the real coin, but it is unknown whether the counterfeit coin is lighter or heavier than the real coin. Please design a efficient algorithm to detect this counterfeit coin.

Solution:
Take six a, b, c, d, e, f from eight coins, and put three to the balance for comparison. Suppose a, b, c are placed on one side, and d, e, f are placed on the other side.

1. $a + b + c > d + e + f$
2. $a + b + c = d + e + f$
3. $a + b + c < d + e + f$

If $a + b + c > d + e + f$, there is a counterfeit coin in one of the six coins, and g, h are real coins. At this time, one coin can be removed from both side. Suppose that c and f are removed. At the same time, one coin at each side is replaced. Suppose the coins b and e are interchanged, and then the second comparison. There are also three possibilities:

1. $a + e > d + b$: the counterfeit currency must be one of a, d. as long as we compare a real currency h with a, we can find the counterfeit currency. If $a > h$, a is a heavier counterfeit currency; if $a = h$, d is a lighter counterfeit currency.

2. $a + e = d + b$: the counterfeit currency must be one of c, f, and the real coin h is compared with c. If $c > h$, c is a heavier counterfeit currency; if $c = h$, then f is a lighter counterfeit currency.

3. $a + e < d + b$: one of b or e is a counterfeit coin , Also use the real coin h to compare with b, if $b > h$, then b is a heavier counterfeit currency; if $b = h$, then e is a lighter counterfeit currency;

Graphic Solution

Heavy   Light

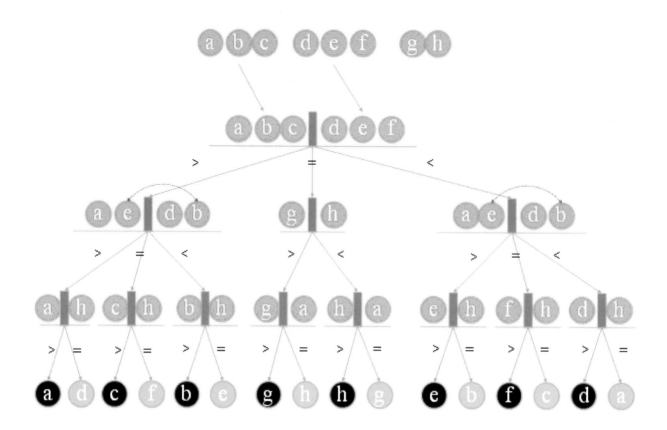

EightCoins.c

```c
#include <stdio.h>
#include<stdlib.h>
#define random(x) (rand()%x)

void compare(int coins[], int i, int j, int k) {//coin[k] true,coin[i]>coin[j]
    if (coins[i] > coins[k]) //coin[i]>coin[j]&&coin[i]>coin[k] ----->coin[i] is a heavy
counterfeit coin
        printf("\nCounterfeit currency %d  is heavier ", (i + 1));
    else //coin[j] is a light counterfeit coin
        printf("\nCounterfeit currency %d  is lighter ", (j + 1));
}

void eightcoins(int coins[]) {
    if (coins[0] + coins[1] + coins[2] == coins[3] + coins[4] + coins[5]){ //(a+b+c)==(d+e+f)
        if (coins[6] > coins[7]) //g>h?(g>a?g:a):(h>a?h:a)
            compare(coins, 6, 7, 0);
        else //h>g?(h>a?h:a):(g>a?g:a)
            compare(coins, 7, 6, 0);
    } else if (coins[0] + coins[1] + coins[2] > coins[3] + coins[4] + coins[5]){ //(a+b+c)>(d+e+f)
        if (coins[0] + coins[3] == coins[1] + coins[4]) //(a+e)==(d+b)
            compare(coins, 2, 5, 0);
        else if (coins[0] + coins[3] > coins[1] + coins[4]) //(a+e)>(d+b)
            compare(coins, 0, 4, 1);
        if (coins[0] + coins[3] < coins[1] + coins[4]) //(a+e)<(d+b)
            compare(coins, 1, 3, 0);
    } else if (coins[0] + coins[1] + coins[2] < coins[3] + coins[4] + coins[5]) {//(a+b+c)<(d+e+f)
        if (coins[0] + coins[3] == coins[1] + coins[4]) //(a+e)>(d+b)
            compare(coins, 5, 2, 0);
        else if (coins[0] + coins[3] > coins[1] + coins[4]) //(a+e)>(d+b)
            compare(coins, 3, 1, 0);
        if (coins[0] + coins[3] < coins[1] + coins[4]) //(a+e)<(d+b)
            compare(coins, 4, 0, 1);
    }
}
```

```
int main()
{
    int coins[8];
    int i;
    // Initial coin weight is 10
    for (i = 0; i < 8; i++)
        coins[i] = 10;

    printf("Enter weight of counterfeit currency  (larger or smaller than 10) :");
    int coin;
    scanf("%d", &coin);
    coins[random(8)] = coin;

    eightcoins(coins);

    for (i = 0; i < 8; i++)
        printf("%d , ", coins[i]);

    return 0;
}
```

Result:

First run:
```
Enter weight of counterfeit currency  (larger or smaller than 10) :
2

Counterfeit currency 2 is lighter
10 , 2 , 10 , 10 , 10 , 10 , 10 , 10 ,
```

Run again:
```
Enter weight of counterfeit currency  (larger or smaller than 10) :
13

Counterfeit currency 4 is heavier
10 , 10 , 10 , 13 , 10 , 10 , 10 , 10 ,
```

Knapsack Problem

Suppose you have a backpack with a weight of up to 8 kg, and you want to the backpack with a total price of Products, suppose the fruit (ID, Name,Price and Weight)

ID	Name	Price	Weight
0	Plum	4kg	4500
1	Apple	5kg	5700
2	Orange	2kg	2250
3	Strawberry	1kg	1100
4	Melon	6kg	6700

Solution:

To solve the optimization problem we can use Dynamic Programming. In the beginning there is a empty set, every time add an element, find the best solution at this stage, until all elements are added. After entering the set finally can get the best solution.

There are two arrays, value and item
value: the total price of the current best solution.
item : the last fruit in the backpack.
there are 8 backpacks with a weight of 1 to 8, and find the best solution for each backpack.

Gradually put the fruit in the backpack and find the best solution:

1. Put in plums:

Weight of Backpack	1kg	2 kg	3 kg	4 kg	5 kg	6 kg	7 kg	8 kg
Value	0	0	0	4500	4500	4500	4500	9000
Item	-	-	-	0	0	0	0	0 , 0
Name	-	-	-	Plum	Plum	Plum	Plum	2* Plum

2. Put in apples:

Weight of Backpack	1kg	2 kg	3 kg	4 kg	5 kg	6 kg	7 kg	8 kg
Value	0	0	0	4500	5700	5700	5700	9000
Item	-	-	-	0	1	1	1	0 , 0
Name	-	-	-	Plum	Apple	Apple	Apple	2* Plum

3. Put in oranges:

Weight of Backpack	1kg	2 kg	3 kg	4 kg	5 kg	6 kg	7 kg	8 kg
Value	0	2250	2250	4500	5700	6750	7950	9000
Item	-	2	2	0	1	0 , 2	1 , 2	0 , 0
Name	-	Orange	Orange	Plum	Apple	Orange Plum	Orange Apple	2* Plum

4. Put in strawberrys:

Weight of Backpack	1kg	2 kg	3 kg	4 kg	5 kg	6 kg	7 kg	8 kg
Value	1100	2250	3350	4500	5700	6800	7950	9050
Item	3	2	2 , 3	0	1	0 , 3	1 , 2	1 , 2 , 3
Name	Strawberry	Orange	Orange Strawberry	Plum	Apple	Plum Strawberry	Orange Apple	Strawberry Orange Apple

5. Put in melons:

Weight of Backpack	1kg	2 kg	3 kg	4 kg	5 kg	6 kg	7 kg	8 kg
Value	1100	2250	3350	4500	5700	6800	7950	9050
Item	3	2	2 , 3	0	1	0 , 3	1 , 2	1 , 2 , 3
Name	Strawberry	Orange	Orange Strawberry	Plum	Apple	Plum Strawberry	Apple Orange	Apple Orange Strawberry

From the last table that when the backpack weighs 8 kg, a maximum of 9050, so the best solution is to put Strawberries, Oranges and Apples, and the total price is 9050.

Knapsack.c

```c
#include <stdio.h>
#include <string.h>
#define MAXSIZE 8
#define MINSIZE 1

struct Fruit
{
    char name[50];
    int size;
    int price;
};

int main()
{
    int item[MAXSIZE + 1] = {0};
    int value[MAXSIZE + 1] = {0};
    struct Fruit fruits[5] = {
            {"Plum", 4, 4500},
            {"Apple", 5, 5700},
            {"Orange", 2, 2250},
            {"Strawberry", 1, 1100},
            {"Melon", 6, 6700}
            };

    int i;
    int j;
    int length;
    length = sizeof(fruits) / sizeof(fruits[0]);
    for (i = 0; i < length; i++)
    {
        for (j = fruits[i].size; j <= MAXSIZE; j++)
        {
            int p = j - fruits[i].size;
            int newValue = value[p] + fruits[i].price;
            if (newValue > value[j])
            { // Find the best solution
                value[j] = newValue;
                item[j] = i;
            }
        }
    }
}
```

```
    printf("Item \t Price \n");
    for (i = MAXSIZE; i >= MINSIZE; i = i - fruits[item[i]].size )
    {
        printf("%s\t %d \n",fruits[item[i]].name, fruits[item[i]].price);
    }
    printf("Total \t %d", value[MAXSIZE]);

    return 0;
}
```

Result:

```
Item        Price
Strawberry  1100
Orange      2250
Apple       5700
Total       9050
```

Josephus Problem

There are 9 Jewish hid in a hole with Josephus and his friends . The 9 Jews decided to die rather than be caught by the enemy, so they decided In a suicide method, 11 people are arranged in a circle, and the first person reports the number. After each number is reported to the third person, the person must commit suicide. Then count again from the next one until everyone commits suicide.But Josephus and his friends did not want to obey. Josephus asked his friends to pretend to obey, and he arranged the friends with himself. In the 2th and 7st positions, they escaped this death game.

Solution:
As long as the array is treated as a ring. Fill in a count for each dataless area, until the count reaches 11, and then list the array from index 1, you can know that each suicide order in this position is the Joseph's position. The 11-person position is as follows:

4 10 1 7 5 2 11 9 3 6 8

From the above, the last two suicide was in the 31st and 16th position. The previous one Everyone died, so they didn't know that Joseph and his friends didn't follow the rules of the game.

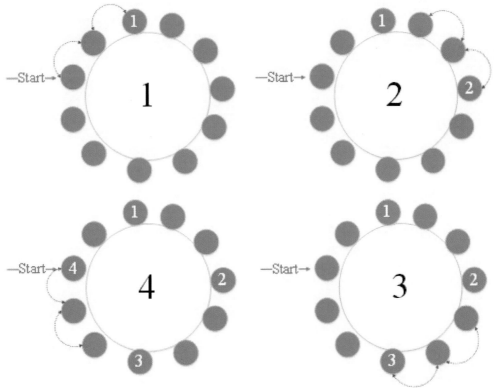

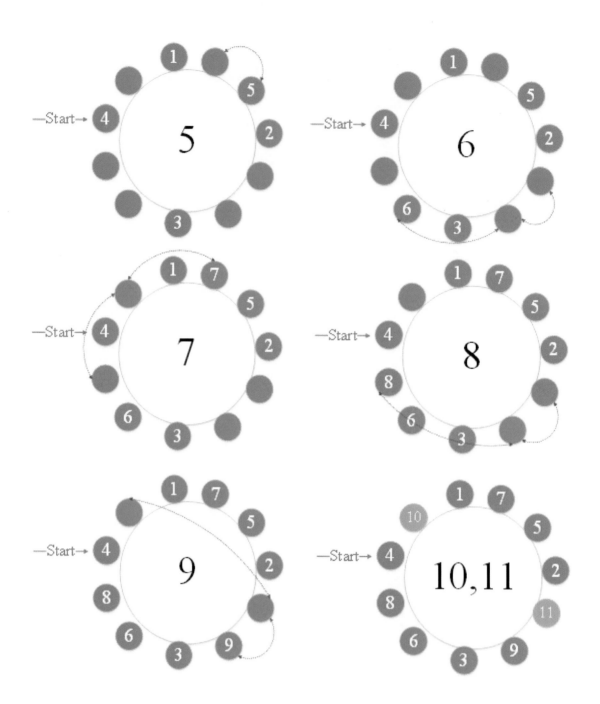

Joseph.c

```c
#include <stdio.h>
#define N 11
#define M 3

int main()
{
    int man[N] = {0};
    int count = 1;
    int i = 0, pos = -1;
    int alive = 0;

    while (count <= N)
    {
        do {
            pos = (pos + 1) % N; // Ring
            if (man[pos] == 0)
                i++;
            if (i == M)
            {
                i = 0;
                break;
            }
        } while(1);
        man[pos] = count;
        count++;
    }
    printf("\nJoseph sequence : ");
    for (i = 0; i < N; i++)
        printf("%d , ", man[i]);

    return 0;
}
```

Result:

```
Joseph sequence:
4 , 10 , 1 , 7 , 5 , 2 , 11 , 9 , 3 , 6 , 8 ,
```

If you enjoyed this book and found some benefit in reading this, I'd like to hear from you and hope that you could take some time to post a review on Amazon. Your feedback and support will help us to greatly improve in future and make this book even better.

You can follow this link now.

http://www.amazon.com/review/create-review?&asin=B08FKQK2FB

Different country reviews only need to modify the amazon domain name in the link:
www.amazon.co.uk
www.amazon.de
www.amazon.fr
www.amazon.es
www.amazon.it
www.amazon.ca
www.amazon.nl
www.amazon.in
www.amazon.co.jp
www.amazon.com.br
www.amazon.com.mx
www.amazon.com.au

I wish you all the best in your future success!

Printed in Great Britain
by Amazon